PRAISE FOR
PLAY A BIGGER GAME

"*Play a Bigger Game* guides readers to unlock their full potential and win at the game of life. This book is a must-read for anyone aspiring to achieve greatness!"

DAVID MELTZER, LEGENDARY SPORTS EXECUTIVE, BESTSELLING AUTHOR, SPEAKER, AND INVESTOR

"No matter where you came from or where you are at, you can play a bigger game in relationships, family, marriage, fatherhood, business, and life. Markus not only gives us the path to play a bigger game with his experience . . . he does it from the North Star of his heart. This book will inspire you to lead with your mind and heart to go big!"

LARRY HAGNER, THREE-TIME AMAZON BESTSELLING AUTHOR, HOST OF *THE DAD EDGE* PODCAST (THE NUMBER ONE DAD PODCAST ON ITUNES AND SPOTIFY)

"Where you are right now is not a life sentence. You can grow, expand, and learn the tools to play a much bigger game. This book speaks to people who know they're here for much more, and it gives them the practical tools to tap into more of their own potential to create a life full of opportunities and fulfillment. Markus is a beacon of hope and inspiration, and this book is a must read."

CRAIG SIEGEL, BESTSELLING AUTHOR, GLOBAL SPEAKER, COACH, PODCAST HOST, AND MARATHONER

"If you want to change your story and play a bigger game, Markus Kaulius will help you rise to your potential. His fun and energetic writing is relatable, inspiring, and useful."

NICK HUTCHISON, FOUNDER OF BOOKTHINKERS AND BESTSELLING AUTHOR OF *RISE OF THE READER*

"If you read *Play a Bigger Game*, you will be inspired. If you take action on the seven principles taught, you will change your story and create a life of abundance! Markus tackles the challenges we ALL face in life with a contagious positivity that will make you want to put these principles into play immediately! He doesn't just talk the talk; he walks the walk. There's no better guide to help you transform!"

DIANA CHALOUX-LACERTE, CO-CEO, HITCH FIT; CO-CEO, SOULFIT RETREATS; AUTHOR; SPEAKER; TWO-TIME WORLD FITNESS CHAMPION

"Markus Kaulius has a zest for life, a track record of success, and a passion for serving others. Read this book and learn how to get to the next level."

RORY VADEN, CO-FOUNDER, BRAND BUILDERS GROUP, AND *NEW YORK TIMES* BESTSELLING AUTHOR OF *TAKE THE STAIRS*

"Passion is a word that gets thrown around too easily; Markus embodies it. He uses his sincere passion for helping others and grounds it with a deep faith, visionary thinking, and a playful style that will give you the motivation and tools to take monumental action in your life as he has."

JOSH LINKNER, FIVE-TIME TECH ENTREPRENEUR, TWO-TIME *NEW YORK TIMES* BESTSELLING AUTHOR, AND VENTURE CAPITAL INVESTOR

"Playing a bigger game is literally impossible without making better decisions faster and taking purposeful action. This playbook is optimized for both. There may be seven principles within, but there are infinite truths—designed to deliver a more fulfilling, successful, and impactful life."

PAUL EPSTEIN, FORMER NFL & NBA EXECUTIVE, TWO-TIME BESTSELLING AUTHOR OF *BETTER DECISIONS FASTER* AND *THE POWER OF PLAYING OFFENSE,* AWARD-WINNING SPEAKER

"Markus has this innate ability to bring you into the place he was mentally during the toughest of times, then show you how he leaned on his faith and pivoted into what he has become today through his seven principles. Markus not only inspires change but provides actionable steps for personal growth. This is a must-read for those looking to level up their lives—so many valuable principles to follow daily."

MICAH LACERTE, CO-CEO, HITCH FIT; CO-CEO, SOULFIT RETREATS; *IRON MAN* COVER MODEL; MUSCLE MODEL WORLD CHAMPION

"Life is all about your mindset. Each day you wake up and you have a choice on how you want to live your life. *Play a Bigger Game* is a road map to success, whether you are trying to be a champion in sports, business, or life. This book will help you win in all aspects."

ANTHONY "SHOWTIME" PETTIS, FORMER UFC AND WEC CHAMPION, INVESTOR, BROADCASTER

amplify

an imprint of Amplify Publishing Group

For more information, please contact:
Amplify Publishing, an imprint of Amplify Publishing Group
620 Herndon Parkway, Suite 220
Herndon, VA 20170
info@amplifypublishing.com

Library of Congress Control Number: 2023922567
CPSIA Code: PRV0124A
ISBN-13: 979-8-89138-007-3

Printed in the United States

FOR BROOKE,

without whom I would not have the strength to enter
the world as I do.

PLAY A
BIGGER GAME

SEVEN UNIVERSAL PRINCIPLES
TO EXPERIENCE
TRUE FULFILLMENT
AND WIN AT LIFE

MARKUS KAULIUS

amplify

an imprint of Amplify Publishing Group

CONTENTS

PROLOGUE

As I walked through the hallway toward our hotel unit, high in the Whaler tower overlooking Kaanapali beach, I heard a horrifying scream coming from inside our room, a scream like I had never heard before.

I burst through the door to see a scene straight out of a movie: a female family member on the wrong side of the balcony railing, threatening to jump.

My father and two other family members on the deck stood at a cautious distance, wailing and pleading for her to step back onto the inside of the railing.

Without losing a split second, I rushed straight at her, grabbed her with all my strength, and threw her back onto the balcony.

I don't know if I did this the "right" way.

I can imagine rushing a person in this position won't always turn out well.

It was my instinct to move as I did, so I won't apologize for it or take credit for the outcome.

This is obviously an extremely traumatic thing for a fifteen-year-old to experience. I can't say for certain all the ways this monumental event impacted my life, but I can tell you that from that moment on I have always been a man who takes action. I don't need all the facts, I don't need a perfect plan, and I don't need to overthink and overanalyze.

The cost of hesitation is too high.

INTRODUCTION

My name is Markus Kaulius, and I have lived a successful life! I started from very humble beginnings—and was a loser in all respects. My parents divorced when I was seven, and the brokenness and lack of love I felt because of it put me on a sad path for many years. Until I changed my story at fifteen, I had only the bare minimum of confidence and self-respect required to stay alive. Until I accepted control over the outcomes in my life, I had no money, no family, and no hope that there was more to life than what I was seeing in front of me. I did not believe I was worthy of respect, success, or love.

As of the writing of this book, I have helped people across the globe lose over three million pounds of fat. I have sat on the boards of many incredible companies. I have taken products from inception to over $170 million in sales. I have married the woman of my dreams (nineteen years and counting) and have two of the most amazing little girls. But I am certain I couldn't have written a single word of this book if I hadn't made a major life correction and turned away from the self-loathing, unconfident, weak boy I told myself that I was. I had to choose to become the high-achieving, self-assured, powerful, confident man I was always meant to be. I didn't like my story, so I changed it.

I wrote this book to help other high achievers who are currently trapped in a shell of the person they were born to be. Some of you may even see success in some areas of your life but wonder why you still have an emptiness or lack of contentment.

If you follow the principles I did, improve your mindset, take concrete action daily, and aim to learn every moment of every day, you will experience more success and true fulfillment than your mind will be able to handle.

"The only thing that's keeping you from getting what you want is the story you keep telling yourself."
—TONY ROBBINS

In the history of humanity, there has never been an easier time to stand out as a high achiever. Today's workforce is the softest it has ever been. Work ethic is lacking. Taking any steps forward can instantly set you apart from the herd. If you read this book, you are in an elite 1 percent of humanity that is taking action to stand out. **If you take my challenges and apply the principles I give you, I have perfect confidence that you and everyone around you will quickly notice a massive difference in who you are, and your life will forever be changed.** If you lean into it and commit yourself to that new life, only your imagination can describe the success you will experience in this lifetime.

Through the techniques I learned in fitness, I will help you train your brain and put you on an unfailing Mind Diet that will have you seeing the world through new eyes immediately. It will be up to you to continue the exercises and maintain a healthy environment for your mind. The result may be more success than you can fathom.

Just as it is with exercise and diet, you can learn about all the right techniques, the right weights to use, the reps, the right and wrong foods, and the rest you need, but if you don't apply the knowledge, nothing in your life is going to change. I will teach you the exercises, how often to do them, and the correct form . . . but you are the one who needs to consistently put in the work to see your life transformed. **Be confident in this: I have never seen someone consistently apply and practice these principles and not see their lives radically change.**

You might not be able to be perfectly consistent—that's okay! No one is saying you have to be. Just as with your eating, there is room for a cheat meal here and there. As long as you get back on it tomorrow, you will be on the right path. **You can strive for perfection, but focus instead on being 1 percent better today than you were yesterday.**

Through these techniques and many others, we will radically amplify your energy. We will find all the ways that energy is spent on things that deserve none, things that weigh us down every minute of every day. We will discuss techniques on how to manage stress and relieve you of your burdens, so you are free to pursue immeasurable success in all areas of your life. These techniques will also grant you far more peace and rest; you will be sleeping far deeper than you're used to.

In short, if you commit to read and live through the principles in this book, your life will be filled with more confidence, passion, strength, excitement, ambition, vigor, focus, and all kinds of success! It happened to me.

But before I tell you how I got to where I am, I'd like to share with you where I started. This is truly a story of "if I can do it, anyone can!"

THE BULLY PARADOX

In the beginning, there was a boy who stood 6'4" and weighed a whopping 120 pounds soaking wet. His name was Mark. At this time in history, the word *mark* was a special kind of insult you would call someone who was a bull's-eye for bullying. Our mark's character reflected the words the bullies spoke about him: he was weak and soft, and he felt undeserving of love or praise. In Mark, you could find no self-confidence, no self-worth, and no joy. This is the type of boy no girl would pay any attention to and no bully could resist. He walked a sad path.

Mark's father had left the family before Mark turned seven, but his father's work had kept him from developing any kind of bond with Mark for years before this. His mother, God bless her, had already raised three children and was forced to go back to school and work to provide. Now, Mark had no relationship with his father *or* his mother.

Mark spent eight to ten hours per day, every day, in his imaginary Lego world or watching TV shows like *Growing Pains, Family Ties, Full House*—shows where the father was an inconceivably awesome man who was always there for his kids. He also loved shows like *Saved by the Bell* and *Cheers*, where the studly man of all men was invincible and his confidence was inescapable. Mark daydreamed of wrapping these characters up into one incredible man—the man he dreamed he would one day be.

THE BIRTH OF MARKUS

When Mark was fifteen, he was fortunate that his father was kind enough to invite Mark on a vacation with his new family. A plane ride to Maui set the stage for the mindset turning point that would forever change this broken boy.

In writing this now, I realize this was the first time I heard directly from God. "No one you're about to meet knows who you are at home. No one knows what is said about you or the names they call you. No one knows that girls don't look at you and that you are picked on constantly. What if you weren't that person? What if the person they meet is full of confidence? What if you are the guy everyone wants to be around? It won't be enough to just put on an act—you need to believe it in your soul. You need to become this new man, and you will need a new name to fit your new persona."

Just as with many men in the Bible who do great things for God, He gave me a new name to signify the death of the old me.

"From this point forward, you will be known as Markus."

I know how dramatic this sounds; I get it. No, I am not Moses, but those words came to me so clearly.

I stepped off the plane five hours later as a different human being. I walked with more confidence. I spoke with confidence and flair! Immediately, girls took notice (I know it's a little strange for me to start with how girls responded, but please remember, I was fifteen and had barely had a girl look in my direction up until this point in my life). I went straight up to the coolest group of teenagers on the beach of Kaanapali, the in-crowd, and made them aware that a new cool guy had landed. There wasn't a moment on the trip when I wasn't invited to hang out with the coolest guys and the most beautiful girls.

I will never forget what one of these beautiful girls said to me on a date—a quote that perfectly captures the shock and wonder of this dramatic mindset change. She said, "I've never met a guy with your level of confidence, but with the body you have," referring to the fact that someone with that skinny and frail of a body had no right to be that confident! I feel like it makes the story even funnier that her name was Charity!

To anyone who says they can't change overnight, I say, "You don't know what you don't know." **I am living proof that once you make a mindset change, your life WILL be different.** No, it isn't as easy as making a declaration—it will require consistent, concrete actions to solidify the change. The first step is to realize it is possible. Before Roger Bannister ran a mile in under four minutes, it was said to be humanly impossible. Because he proved that it was possible, many others were able to accomplish that impossible feat—including John Landy, just weeks later.

I have shown you that it can be done. Keep reading for the steps to make your life change happen. You can be my John Landy. Yes, this was the same trip that God used me to grab that family member who was on the wrong side of the balcony railing. I am confident that if I hadn't made these changes to myself before I landed in Maui, the end of that story could have been very different. Imagine the cost if I had not made these changes to my life. What will be the cost to your life if you don't make these changes today?

> "A prophet is not without honor except in his own town . . . "
> —MARK 6:4

As I write this, for the first time I see God's incredible plans for this verse in my life. Mark 6:4—pertaining to

Mark Kaulius, at **6'4"**, who was on his way home to a place where he had no honor, no respect, no love.

On the plane ride home, I was met with a scary realization: no one at home knows that I am cool now! Praise God for giving me the strength to realize this new me was the only me, and the old me was gone. Of course, most people weren't willing to accept that truth, but I was blessed with new strength to turn away from those people. Know this: **when you make your extraordinary change, there will be many people who prefer you as weak and average.** These people won't accept the new you. Their own insecurities would prefer you go back to the old you to appease them. They don't want the best for your life, so you may need to move on from them and keep them as a special memory from an old chapter.

I must caveat this last statement. First, give people time to come to terms with the new you. You will need to offer patience and mercy if they don't immediately embrace you. This will require increased communication—don't be afraid to talk it out. Second, if you are married, I am not suggesting you leave your spouse because they don't accept the new you. Ideally, you married someone who wants the best for you—but some of you didn't; your changes will require some serious communication and sometimes some counseling. In a later chapter, I will walk you through the best steps to get family members on board with the new you and the critical actions and statements to avoid if you ever want them to come around.

Without knowing it at the time, I had begun my new Mind Diet and exercises. I had made the decision to change, but the real work had just begun. The diet began with cleansing my life of the negative people who didn't want to accept this far better version of me, Markus. It continued with daily practices that kept my mind focused on what the new me should be doing and how a studlier version of me would act. **The exercises I needed to do daily are the very exercises I share in this book.** I don't pretend that I knew all of this at such a young age, but just as you will start your journey with my tips and experience great success, you will also read more books and pick up new tips along the way. This new you journey will be ever evolving, and it starts today!

WHAT DO I DO WITH THIS NEW POWER?

This might be the most exciting information I get to share with you! You have made the realization that you were meant for more in this world than what your critics have told you, and you are ready to move forward in this new life. But in what direction do you go? First, recognize the freedom you feel in this moment and know that if you start down a new path and don't love it, you get more than one shot at a new life! You can come back to this same spot and try again—you do not have to default back to your old life if the first new path you try isn't the winner. **What makes this moment so exciting is the fact that you get to write your own story right now.**

If the idea of being an insurance salesman sounds like a prison sentence, don't write yourself in as an insurance salesman! (No offense to all you insurance salespeople—I have tons of friends who sell insurance and I have loads of respect for the profession!) What lights your fire? What are you excited to talk about, to take part in, to experience? No matter what your answer is, there is someone making a living doing that as their "job." The next chapter of your life is currently a blank page; don't let the silly things of this world produce fear in you over that blankness. That page should excite you because you get to write it exactly how you want to write it. **You are the star of this story; don't write yourself in as an extra!**

This is where your trust in God will play a major role. I understand that many of you reading this aren't there yet, so please consider this an invitation to discover our creator. If you are lacking in trust, this is a beautiful way to build it up. First, know that He wants what is best for you.* He loves you and will not put you in a job you hate, especially if you are asking Him what career path you should follow. Take time each day to ask Him to guide you. He will answer you, but you need to be watching, listening, and patient.

Please take out a notebook and a pen. I want you to start by writing fifteen to twenty things you love doing. These are the things that you could work on for hours without noticing the time fly by.

This is brainstorming time, so please bring no negativity into this process. If you love playing video games for hours, write down *video games*. If you love hiking or being in nature, write it down. Fun fact: I know many people who make a fortune playing video games for a living. I also have friends who make a great living hiking outdoors.

Now I'd like you to write down fifteen to twenty professions that interest you. Again, this is brainstorming time, so allow yourself to get creative and put down a bunch of random professions before you criticize any of them. Pretend you are five years old and start listing

---

* Luke 11:11–13. [11] "Which of you fathers, if your son asks for a fish, will give him a snake instead? [12] Or if he asks for an egg, will give him a scorpion? [13] If you then, though you are evil, know how to give good gifts to your children, how much more will your Father in heaven give the Holy Spirit to those who ask him!"

away. A five-year-old would never say, "You can't do that" or "What about the mortgage?" (That said, I suggest you stay in reality and don't write down that you want to be a fire engine.)

Do you notice anything from the first list that matches anything from the second list? These jobs might be worth exploring and having some conversations with friends about. Here's my favorite part of this exercise—just taking the time to do this exercise has now opened your mind to new possibilities. Just fifteen minutes ago, many people reading this believed the job they have right now is the only job they might ever have. Now look at you; you are seriously pondering if there is some type of job around playing video games! (Can you believe how many millionaires have been created through playing video games? Who saw that coming?!)

Let's open up your mind a bit more. Your brain likely tried to start finding connections to jobs that would allow you to quit yours tomorrow to follow your passion. I love that, and I am excited for you that you are on that path. But keep in mind that creating revenue from one, or many, of these passions can start as a side hustle.

I have so much respect for people who start their side hustle while keeping their job. Not only did they create extra income, but in many instances the side hustle grew to a point where they knew that if they did it full-time, they would make more than they were currently making, plus they would have a much better quality of life—that's when they quit their day job.

MY FIRST SIDE HUSTLE

When I was in university, I read a business case study about Wendy's restaurants that changed my life! In this case study, a Wendy's customer got on the phone one day and didn't stop calling and charming her way through until she got the CEO on the phone. This blew my mind. How could a normal person get the CEO of a major corporation on the phone? I had created a barrier in my mind between what is and isn't possible, and that barrier was clearly not reality. **What other limits have I put on my life that don't exist outside my self-construct?** What levels could I reach in life if I learned to wield such power? That was a Tuesday afternoon.

Tuesday night, as I laid my head on the pillow, I saw a full, beautiful business plan that involved my biggest passion. On Wednesday, I got on the phone with the intent of calling enough times and charming enough people to get the "yes" I was after. It took only one phone call! I was able to get through to the CEO of a sports nutrition distribution company. I explained to him how much I loved his supplements and how I would make his life better if he allowed me to sell them (even though selling to someone like me, without a store, was 100 percent against policy). His initial answer was a firm "no chance." But I knew this was a great plan and that I would bring great value to this man's life and business, so I kept him on the line until he conceded. **I told him that I would be his greatest success story. (Fun side note: I was!)**

On Thursday, I had $10,000 of his supplements beautifully displayed on my bedroom wall. On Friday, I received another $5,000 from my second-favorite company (whose CEO also said yes). This $15,000 was every penny I had to my name. On Saturday morning, I had my first sale.

For the next few years, I was the supplement guy! Friends told friends that I was the hookup and people dropped by day and night. The memories I have of strangers sitting on my bed as I educated them on supplementation will always make me smile. My friends called me the Healthy Drug Dealer!

This was my side hustle while I went through university. I also kept my serving job, as I was determined to put money away for whatever crazy business idea I would have next.

The warehouse/bedroom of a university-age "Healthy Drug Dealer."

BEING A MENTOR

My brother Darren is a life coach. He is truly amazing at it. He guides people through their mental barriers and allows their best version to come out. We had a beautiful discussion last week about the difference between a coach and a mentor. He helped me see that a coach is there to get the best out of you by reaching in and drawing out the best of what is in you. **A coach will encourage, direct, and push you toward greatness.** A coach allows the client to be the hero and helps them find the answer within themselves. He added that a coach shouldn't be the one to answer the big questions. Why? "Because a coach is someone who can teach it but hasn't necessarily done it. A mentor has done it and done it well."

I loved the simplicity of Darren's answer. While of course some coaches may have already "done it," I'm going to use Darren's definition because it separates the two cleanly. Before we discuss what mentoring means to us, I want to say how valuable I believe coaches are. I have used coaches and mentors for many years. My brother has coached me for some time now, and I can confidently say that I would not be where I am without him.

By the same definition, a mentor has been there and done that. A mentor has traveled the path and is now laying out the map for others to follow. These definitions helped put into perspective the areas in life I can mentor—and areas where maybe I shouldn't. It is because of this understanding that as I write this book, I will often be speaking to and using the language of the male reader.

For the female readers, I mean zero disrespect. I love and appreciate the women in my life. I was raised in a house of women (one mom, two sisters), and I now live in a house of women (one wife, two daughters, and one female budgie). I want to see women rise in business just as much as—or more than—men. I have two daughters, and I want to see them blow the roof off. I hope female readers will utilize every principle in this book to great success. But I have to recognize that women face unique challenges that I am not equipped to address. (To offer one example, I have never been overlooked for promotion due to my boss's fear that I might get pregnant.)

I am excited and honored to share with all of you, both men and women, everything I have learned and the principles that will change the course of your life.

WHERE DO WE GO FROM HERE?

I have seven principles I live by: Integrity, Choice, Faith, Service, Gratitude, Discipline, and Consistency. This is the 24/7 Philosophy—these seven principles have the power to change your life in twenty-four hours.

The rest of the book is devoted to sharing these principles and giving you guidance in applying them to your life. I so appreciate that you have come this far with me, and I promise that if you read these principles, stop to think about how you can apply them, and put effort into the exercises I give you, you will change your life and experience more success in every area. **With my full confidence, I tell you that your life will change.** Your dreams will not necessarily come true overnight, but by tomorrow you will be able to notice a difference in yourself and recognize the freedom and positive feelings that come with taking real steps and putting in effort to become the person you were made to be.

I will not only help you achieve more success in your life, but I will also help you recognize your growth and find joy in it. Far too often we see people attain their goals (often financial), only to find no added joy in the achievement. Sadly, in many cases it leads to a deep emptiness and disillusionment because they were sure they would find happiness at the end of this journey. I will help you lay the foundation to create success the right way, with the right focus and purpose, and hopefully, if you follow the plan, you will find great joy in the journey and the growth in your life. The other stuff—finances, power, accolades, etc.—will simply be bonuses that you can use to further your growth and satisfaction in helping others.

INTEGRITY

Def.
The quality of being honest and having strong moral
principles; moral uprightness.
The state of being whole and undivided.

For me, integrity is the lens through which all decisions must be made. Asking the question, "What would integrity have me do?" answers 95 percent of all my questions. Integrity, by definition, is an all-or-nothing lifestyle. **There is no 99 percent integrity**.

If you choose to commit to a life of integrity, that focus will motivate you through tough times, give you confidence and assurance in your actions, quickly make you a human of character, and set you apart from the vast majority of the world. It begins with a decision, then comes the work.

Becoming a man of integrity will take time and will require constant attention and focus. This world is designed for, and encourages you to be, someone without integrity, so you must keep your guard up at all times. You will face millions of challenges in your life where, at first glance and with short-term thinking, the "no integrity" path is easier. In the short term, it is often easier to tell a lie than to face up to the truth. You might experience more pleasure eating that cake or cheating on your spouse in the short term. Most temptations seem like the best path . . . short-term.

One of our generation's greatest businessmen and the founder of Apple, Steve Jobs, often spoke about integrity and why living a life of integrity is the only way.

> When you're a carpenter making a beautiful chest of drawers, you're not going to use a piece of plywood on the back, even though it faces the wall and nobody will ever see it. You'll know it's there, so you're going to use a beautiful piece of wood on the back. For you to sleep well at night, the aesthetic, the quality, has to be carried all the way through.

In this section, I will help you construct a life of integrity. Because of the pitfalls set up to derail us from that life and the constant temptations trying to pull us in a different direction, it is imperative that you see this lifestyle as a perpetual work in progress and celebrate the wins of the journey. We must learn to recognize the benefits of this lifestyle any time they arise to further remind us that we have chosen the right path. Let me encourage you with this: **the longer you stay true to this path and the more you build strength in it and routines around it, it does become easier to stay with it.**

If you fall off the path at any time, you can step right back up. Make sure to take enough time in your mind to learn the lesson and recognize the cost of your misstep; but once that lesson has been engrained, move forward and don't look back. **Errors happen, but if you choose to spend the rest of your life questioning the error and not forgiving yourself for it, you will not live up to the potential**

I know you have in you. Every drop of energy you spend on guilt could have been used on moving forward and getting ahead.

A life of integrity comes with more benefits than I could ever express in one book. The longer you live with this integrity, the more influence, admiration, wisdom, confidence, strength, character, and ultimately success you will gain in all areas of your life.

NO ASSUMPTIONS, NO PRIDE, NO LIES

> "Pride comes before the fall."
> —PROVERBS 16:18

The human brain creates a file for every situation, and that file won't change until you re-open it. We created many files when we were very young, and those defined the world around us as we grew: how you should look, how you do look, what your wife should look like, how much money you should have in the bank, what you should do if someone disrespects you, etc. We forever compare our current state to those files. Sometimes these files serve us—like that file that reminds us that we shouldn't touch a hot stove. But sadly, most of our files are so outdated that they negatively impact our lives every day without our knowing it.

Markus's Example: I have received a specific, wonderful compliment from people many times over the last twenty years. A friend will say something like, "Markus, you have an athletic, lean, muscular physique." What a beautiful compliment, right? For close to twenty years, those words made me feel a sadness when I heard them. Why? Because when I first started working out, I was an ultra-skinny kid with no confidence whose goal was to look very muscular. Here's the funniest part: I don't even like that "very muscular" look and never have, but I created that file before I knew anything about working out. So instead of taking that wonderful compliment and letting it create joy in me for the whole day, it made me sad because it didn't match what my fifteen-year-old self thought I should look like. When I finally recognized this was happening, I updated the file, and now this compliment fills my bucket big time!

"Tennis, anyone?" Here I am in my ultra-skinny teenage days.

I have created a habit: **whenever I am making a decision, I ask if my decision was based on any assumptions** (files that were created long ago but may be outdated, or files created from something I may have heard in passing). The first time I did this simple verification, I realized how many assumptions go into making every little decision in our lives. In my experience, over 90 percent of the assumptions are invalid, outdated, or based on no real facts. One of the saddest realizations I have come to is recognizing how many assumptions were based on something I saw on social media and took as solid fact. Yes, that is incredibly embarrassing to admit, but social media was designed to take over our minds; does it really shock you to think that after spending 10,000 hours on it, it has steered your opinions?

CHALLENGE

When you make your decisions today, ask yourself if each decision is based on any assumptions. Even the simplest decisions we make might be based on outdated or incorrect information. Example: I am going to eat cereal for breakfast. Do you *want* cereal for breakfast? Does cereal sound like a good start to your day or provide the nutrition you desire? Or were you going to reach for cereal because years ago, when you had far less information on health and had different requirements for breakfast, you chose cereal as your go-to breakfast?

Look at the major assumptions at play . . . and you haven't even gotten out of bed yet!

ADVANCED CHALLENGE

Not only will you accept the above challenge and question your assumptions, but you will also force yourself to try new paths. It has been proven that taking a new route to work, adding a walk to your day, eating a new food, etc. will create new neural pathways. Use this opportunity to get your brain fired up today.

PRIDE WILL HINDER YOUR SUCCESS

Pride is what stops us from learning. When I started living by the motto of "I have no pride," I opened up my mind to learn from everyone and in every situation. My mind is constantly looking to learn and update old files. I don't just learn from the people doing it right; I can also learn a ton from the people doing it wrong! Pride and ego will get in the way of this learning by saying, "I am better than that person, so they can't teach me anything." Sadly, you won't learn anything precisely because you have told your brain not to.

Having no pride has also served me incredibly well in my business journey. Having no pride allows me to apologize more often, even when I know I am only a tiny bit at fault. No pride means I am truly open to hearing the other side of any story, and it has taught me that there are multiple ways to see any event (instead of just focusing on the way I saw things).

No pride ultimately means that I am admitting that I am not always right. This isn't the 1950s anymore—a man can admit to not having all the answers, to not always being right, and he can still be a man! In fact, I have found the more I admit that, the better my relationships have become. People appreciate vulnerability. Admitting I don't have all the answers allows people to see me as human and, I believe, has helped get them on my team.

Fun Story

This is my favorite story about how a lack of pride saved a significant investment. I was doing a speaking event for a big client in downtown Toronto. I had around sixty high-value guests who would be in attendance. I spent roughly $25,000 on this night. It was created to feed my guests, spend some quality time with them, win them over to trusting me and my brand, and educate them on how to sell our product effectively. I have done hundreds of these events, and they have always been one of my favorite parts of the job.

The hotel was taking care of everything except the projection screen. I am a principled man, and gouging me for $600 to rent a $100 screen for four hours is just not okay. Remember, I grew up very poor. There are just certain things I can't accept paying $600 for! (Is that just me?) So Amazon delivered the $100 screen to my hotel. All I had to do was carry it to the conference room.

I did not realize the box was going to be eight feet long. It was decently light (maybe 35 pounds) so no big deal, but eight feet is awkwardly long, and you need to be mindful of what you might hit with it! In the elevator, I had to very carefully wedge it in on an angle and take up the whole space. In the lobby, I met one of my guests, and we walked together toward the conference room. As we boarded the escalator, I was able to stand the projector box upright beside me, and we dove into conversation (remember, the whole point is for me to impress my guests, leave a great impression, and give them assurance that I am a good guy who can be trusted).

Did you know there is a certain level of sound that we rarely hear and that when we do, our brains instinctively know something catastrophic has happened? The sound of the box crashing through the low roof over the escalator made me think I was toppling the whole building. Huge chunks of roof fell on my head and all around me.

Fortunately, my default facial expression was shock with a little "you better laugh this off somehow, bro!" But to make me look even more cool, this eight-foot-long box with a built-strong projection screen inside was now stuck between the roof and the escalator stairs, which of course were still moving up—and with each movement up came the loud scraping of the box and a huge thud as it dropped down to the next stair.

I "calmly" tried to pull it out, but the box was at least one foot deep inside the roof, and there was not one foot of room to pull it down. I tried three or four times and didn't move it an inch. The noise and debris were starting to draw more eyes, so I accepted that I had to either make a major move or frantically cry, "Someone please stop the escalator!" So in one big motion, I kicked the bottom out hard and yanked down with all my might. More ceiling, more noise, and more shock filled the lobby. Finally, the box was free. I got to the top, looked my client in the eye, laughed, and said, "Wow, do we have a story to tell!"

I thanked God at that moment that I do not get embarrassed. Pride would tell me how foolish I must have looked. Pride would tell me that this client was going to tell everyone what a clown I am. Pride would have me cower when I had a major dinner and presentation to put on. But how would that help? How would that serve me? Is that the best way to use my energy?

I went on to have one of my best presentations ever and earned one of my favorite stories to tell! The client did tell her superior about the incident, but she framed it in a positive light, telling him how it didn't faze me. We all laughed hard about the ridiculous situation.

CHALLENGE

Watch for an opportunity today to check your pride at the door. If this is a totally new concept to you, I recommend writing sticky notes to remind you of "no pride" and placing them everywhere! It doesn't hurt to set a phone reminder to go off a few times in your day so you are watching for opportunities. After you have tested it out, take a few minutes to analyze how it went. How did others respond? How did you feel about the encounter? How would it have gone differently if your pride and ego had been running the show as usual? I am confident that you will love the outcome and want this to be your new default position.

ADVANCED CHALLENGE

Take part in the above challenge, but now write down each encounter in your day where you allowed your pride and ego to be silenced. Now share with someone (your mastermind group, your spouse, or a close friend) how it went and how it felt. This open dialogue will more firmly solidify your new path and encourage you to stay on it. It will also deepen your relationship with whomever you share it with, as they will see you opening up and may want to be a supporter of your self-improvement. (Do keep in mind, though, that some people will not support you in your self-improvement. I will help you with that kind of communication in Chapter 2.)

NO LIES

If you want to live a life marked by integrity, you must commit to a 100 percent no-lie policy. When I first made this decision, I was naïve enough to think there were likely only a few lies per year I would need to remove from my life. Sadly, "little white lies" had become a part of my journey. I put those in quotes because a lie is a lie, no matter what kind of cute words you try to sugarcoat it with! Lies are more deceptive than we realize. **What we think will help us**

or get us out of a tricky situation will inevitably entangle us in a web that will never let us free. This is an all-or-nothing situation— let's go for zero lies.

A quick reminder of the obvious: **a lie never ends with just one lie.** You will need to create other lies to support the first. Living a life dedicated to integrity and zero lies frees you of all the deception, negative feelings, guilt, storytelling, etc. and allows your mind to be free to follow your new, healthy, positive path. You never again need to spend energy worrying about what lie you told someone or if you will eventually be found out for the liar you are.

Fun Story

I will never forget the first time I was challenged by this no-lie focus in business and the incredible payoff I got for sticking to integrity. I had forgotten to place a client's order with my team. I found the order two days later and ran down to quickly get it processed and shipped. I called my client, who immediately said he was surprised the order hadn't arrived. He really needed it! For a brief moment, I considered blaming the warehouse. I could say they were behind or that they misplaced the order. Maybe my client would never be the wiser. But integrity had me tell him the truth, and I added that the screwup was actually a good thing! "I screwed up, and I am extremely disappointed in myself. This was 100 percent my fault. Now I owe you a big one. I am going to be extra sensitive with your orders; I am going to add shaker cups and extra samples where I can; and I am going to over-service you because I want to make it up to you."

My client was upset and disappointed, but said he understood. He called two days later and told me how much he respected my owning the error and not lying about it. Believe it or not, this was a turning point in my relationship with this client. It was the moment we turned from a supplier-client relationship to an actual friendship.

Here's the best part—**when you start living a truly 100 percent lie-free life, you will experience a dramatic, positive change in who you are.** I will start by saying this will take time and it will not be easy, but it will be worth it. In the process of removing the lies from your life and owning up to the truth of every situation, you are going to ruffle some feathers. This will cause some seriously uncomfortable conversations and possibly some real hurt in your relationships. That discomfort and pain will force you to start living a better life if you allow it to and if you stay focused on the no-lie policy. In order to avoid those conversations and that pain, you will have to start making better decisions. You are giving your conscience the reins and saying, "I guess you're in charge now!" You will quickly start looking further into your plans and seeing where the issues will likely come up. Maybe a trip to Vegas with those unmarried guys is not a good idea!

"I'm not upset that you lied to me, I'm upset that from now on I can't believe you."
– FRIEDRICH NIETZSCHE

CHALLENGE

Catch yourself today before you lie. Choose to tell the truth and see how it goes. Analyze how it went. How did you feel about choosing the truth? Do you feel more freed or plagued by the truth? How did it make the other person feel? How will that person feel long-term?

ADVANCED CHALLENGE

Take the above challenge and write down the results for a week. This will get you closer to making this no-lie policy a routine. You will feel a great sense of freedom. After a week, telling the truth will already become second nature and will start taking less effort. Continue to analyze the situations and the feelings of everyone involved. You are now on a path toward real integrity and a truly better life!

BEING AUTHENTICALLY YOU

"He is a wise man who does not grieve for the things which he has not, but rejoices for those which he has."
– EPICTETUS

One of the greatest lies we started telling ourselves at a young age is that we want to "fit in." What a bizarre world we live in where we are taught as children to fall in line, act and obey as everyone else, and follow the exact same schedule as every other child. It is no wonder we feel so out of place when we don't want to pay attention during science or if we don't love cooking class. We automatically try to be someone we are not, and anything that makes us unique is perceived as very bad.

At some point in our teens, some of us realize that uniqueness is what makes us awesome! These are the traits God gave you to be the one and only you. **The more you pursue your unique giftings, attributes, and passions, the more you will flourish in life.** I am here to tell you to be unapologetically YOU!

To make the challenge even trickier, with the advent of streaming services and social media, we now have marketers and algorithms working around the clock to have us once again fall in line as adults. Do you know someone who spends more than two hours per day on Netflix and/or social media? More than five? Is that someone you? I hope you see this as the greatest wake-up call of your life and make the decision today to fast from these vices and start to recall who you were before they put you to sleep.

When I was discovering who I was, I had a hypothesis I decided to test out. What if the unique stuff in my head, the stuff I deemed crazy talk, was actually what would draw people to me? To test the hypothesis, I started letting it out for people to see and experience. Before I did, I made sure I thought a little about the reactions I wanted to see and what I would consider valuable data. Not everyone liked what they saw, but when I did get a negative response, it was always from people I didn't really want to be around anyway. The people I liked and wanted to spend time with were more drawn to me than ever. And of course these positive reactions and outcomes to me being my true self reinforced and encouraged me to follow this path even deeper.

What makes you uniquely you is what you have been put on this planet to share. Being yourself will draw the right people to befriend you, the right jobs to find you, the right spouse to be attracted to you, and your unique purpose to be lived out.

CHALLENGE

Watch for opportunities to let people see more of the real you today. Is there a side of you that you keep hidden for fear of judgment? Let me encourage you with the knowledge that everyone has that stuff! You should share it today. I want to remind you to watch for this opportunity in your tight group—the people you care about and who you know care about you. I am confident they will respond positively as you start to share a little more about what makes you uniquely you.

ADVANCED CHALLENGE

Take notes on how the challenge went. These notes are so valuable for reflecting on to remind you to keep being you. Take note of who was drawn closer to you and who seemed to push back. I am confident you will be writing down the answers to exactly whom you should and shouldn't be spending your time with.

This world was blessed with only one of you—please don't deprive us any longer of who you really are—that is the person who will have a major impact on many lives. If you are going to live a lie-free life, start by being truthful about who you really are.

My friend and mentor Ed Mylett talks about being and loving yourself in this way:

> If you don't think you're beautiful, if you don't think you're wonderful, you can't even enjoy the best places in life. The key is we can't love ourselves unless we're being ourselves. The first step to transforming how you feel about, love, and believe in yourself is to truly *be* yourself. To start acting in accordance with your values and beliefs, taking

real actions toward your biggest dreams. The real authentic steps to treat other people in a fashion that's congruent with your character and beliefs. You'll find you will begin to transform into someone you love. You will love yourself when you're being yourself.[*]

"If you want to win in life, you have to be your own biggest fan."
– ED MYLETT

KNOW YOUR WHY

"People don't buy what you do, they buy why you do it."
– SIMON SINEK

Knowing your why is everything! How can you know where you're going without knowing your why? How will you get out of bed tomorrow if you don't know why you are getting out of bed? How do you expect people to follow you, buy from you, trust you, love you if they don't know your why?

Your WHY is your guiding force. Know your why and reflect on it often. You should be able to give a solid elevator pitch on your why to anyone you meet. That twenty-second pitch should tell someone what you are all about, why you are who you are, and why you do what

---

* Mylett, Ed (@edmylettfanpage). 2020. Facebook post, March 5, 2020. https://www.facebook.com/watch/?v=1082362482110217.

you do. Your why will also hold you accountable. **Every action you take should be in line with your why**—if it isn't, why are you doing it?

Your why must go far deeper than the surface stuff. If your why lacks depth ("Because I really want to be a millionaire!") it won't be strong enough to get you through challenging times, which will come. Why do you need that money? Your why might be "I want to make enough money to send my brother and sisters to university" or "I want to pay off my mom's house because she has done so much for me." That's a why.

I have worked with many people whose why was too shallow ("I want to be rich"), and it inevitably left them unfulfilled. Without depth to our why, the achievement of the one goal might come at great cost to other areas in our lives. How many people reach financial or career success at the cost of their family's joy? Or their health? Or all their relationships? This is why it is so important to take time to think through our focus and goals and know what we are or are not willing to sacrifice to achieve.

Your why needs to be specific. If your why is too general ("Because I want to make a difference in the world.") there will be nothing to grip onto and your compass won't work. Your why might be "I want to provide clean drinking water to every child in Africa" or "I want to end starvation in my community."

But most importantly, your why needs to be personal and unique to you, your upbringing, your beliefs, and your story. While providing clean drinking water to the children of Africa is a beautiful and noble cause, if you have no ties to Africa, your connection to this goal might quickly break.

Your why will likely evolve along the way. It is important to take time regularly to make sure you still want to be on the path you are on. Since we live in an instant gratification world now, I must add this: Have you given your why enough time? Are you moving on too soon? Big goals and great achievements take time—get yourself mentally prepared to endure.

AN EXERCISE TO FIND YOUR WHY

Many of you will know right away what your why is, but everyone will benefit from going through these exercises to discover or solidify their why. You will find space to write your answers below. Please give me at least five answers to each question.

What gets you out of bed in the morning? (Think deep here, not just "my job.")

_____

_____

_____

_____

_____

When do you feel most lit up in life (most excited, most full of energy and joy)?

_____

_____

_____

_____

_____

What injustices in the world impact you most? (Do any sadden you to the core?)

_____

_____

_____

_____

_____

Now I'd like to help you solidify a strong why. A weak why is a good start, but it won't have that strength to endure as challenges arise. **A strong why will get you up early, keep you up late, have you acting possessed by your determination to make your dream a reality.** Below are examples of weak vs. strong whys. I left space for you to add your own wants and whys. Feel free to start with a weaker why, then challenge yourself to get deeper and create strength in yours.

WANT	WEAK WHY	STRONG WHY
More money	So I can buy more stuff	So I can buy my mom a house in a safe neighborhood
More time	So I can relax and vacation more	So I can develop a bond with my daughter
More energy	So I can do more	So I can be present and energetic with my family
More respect	So people will do what I say	So I can lead people to make real change in our community

CONFIDENCE

> "Your work is going to fill a large part of your life, and the only way
> to be truly satisfied is to do what you believe is great work. And
> the only way to do great work is to love what you do. If you haven't
> found it yet, keep looking. Don't settle. As with all matters of the
> heart, you'll know when you find it."
> – STEVE JOBS

I know that confidence is something most successful people have in common (at the very least, they are confident in the business that made them successful). I also know that confidence is high on everyone's list of things they would like to improve about themselves. This is why I have included a section about confidence under every principle in this book. **Every principle, when applied properly, will have a dramatically positive impact on your confidence.**

I don't think I need to take too much time to convince you that once you know your why, are on your path to being authentically you, and have rid your life of the white lies and pride, that you will naturally be more confident about the path you are on. **True integrity breeds real confidence.**

Confidence comes from a belief in yourself and knowing that what you are doing is what you are meant to be doing. I call this *alignment*. This book is dedicated to helping you believe in yourself and recognize the amazing gifts you have at your disposal, and to encourage you to share those gifts with the world and trust in the path you have in front of you. This book was created to build your confidence.

In changing the story you tell, inserting extra confidence can be easier than you think. Please take fifteen seconds to close your eyes and picture an extremely confident person. What do you notice about them? Are their shoulders slouched or rolled back? Is their eye contact strong or evasive? Is their breathing erratic or calm and collected? Is their handshake strong or limp? Write down the top ten characteristics you can see about this person. Now go to the mirror and pretend you embody those ten characteristics. Make strong eye contact with yourself. Pull those shoulders back and extend your hand for a strong, confident shake. Was that not far more convincing than you thought it would be? Now if you were able to convince yourself even a little bit, imagine how much more convincing you will be to someone who doesn't know you.

I need to make one point about this whole exercise very clear: You are not pretending to be someone you are not. **You are unleashing the person that you really are.** There is a massive difference, especially when it ties to your integrity. This new, confident version of yourself is the REAL you, the you who has been imprisoned by a bad story for a long time. There is no need to look back any further at the old version, only know that this more confident version of yourself is the one you want behind the wheel.

CHALLENGE

Take this new "character" you have created for a test drive today! Experiment with having your shoulders back, speaking with boldness, breathing calmly . . . and take note of how people respond. I am confident there will be many people who say something like, "Wow, who is this new person in front of me?!"

Please remember that **confidence is a magnet**. We are all drawn to people with confidence because it is rare to see it in our world today. We all believe a confident person knows who they are and where they are going. We put our trust in them, almost blindly, because that confidence suggests they will do better as a leader than the rest of us. That can be you!

Doing the daily exercises on confidence will improve your confidence daily and put your old self more and more to rest. As you receive and absorb the benefits of your newfound confidence, let it sink in and further encourage you to step more boldly into your new persona. Embrace the rewards that come with your confidence and be hungry for more. Every exercise and challenge you find in this book will further enhance your confidence. The more you know who you are, what you are about, what drives you, and where you are going, you will naturally exude more confidence and the world will be excited to follow you.

REDEFINING SUCCESS

"Try not to become a man of success, but rather become a man of value."
– ALBERT EINSTEIN

Your definition of success needs to be examined. As we discussed previously, your definition of success is a file you likely created long ago and haven't taken a second look at. For many years of my life, success meant wearing a red Hawaiian shirt and driving a convertible

Ferrari! Of course, it wouldn't be real success unless I was able to grow that manly moustache too. (For those of you too young, I am referring to the ultra-manly Magnum PI Tom Selleck, who oozed confidence and manliness. Clearly, at a young age I put his image at the peak of "what success looks like"!)

Because success (a wonderfully vague and all-encompassing term) is the end goal for every reader of this book, it is critical that we examine our own definition of success and make it a regular exercise to re-evaluate it to keep us focused on the correct target.

Let's find out if your file on success is outdated. Start by using the space below to write words or short phrases on what success means to you. Try to get at least ten answers. The more detail you can give, the better. Again, please don't filter these answers, just let the words flow and write them down, even if they sound silly to you. We can dissect them after.

Some categories you might want to define success for:

Marriage: What does the relationship look like? What does your spouse look like? What activities do you do together? How does your spouse treat you? How do you make your spouse feel?

Children: How many do you have? What are they like? What are they interested in? What is your relationship like? Are they respectful? Are they disciplined?

Career: What do you do? How many hours do you work? Who are the people you get to work with? How much do you make? What are your clients like? How much stress do you experience from your career?

Health: How do you feel? How do you look? Do you have exercises that you enjoy? What do you eat? How is your sleep?

Stress: How much do you have? How do you deal with it?
Spirituality: Where do you find your peace? How is your relationship with your creator? Do you have a community?
Finances: How much money do you have? What does your house look like? What kind of car do you drive? What is an amazing vacation to you?

Did you notice I didn't ask about wealth until the end? Sadly, this is often the first subject brought up when discussing success. Question: If you had everything in the list above financial where you wanted it to be, would you consider yourself "successful"? I would hope your answer is "YES, extremely successful!" In my humble opinion, wealth has nothing to do with true success and always confuses our vision of what it means to be successful. There is nothing wrong with being financially motivated to a degree, but it is so important to keep it in context, especially when it comes to these other six categories.

What is even wilder is that if you did master all of the above categories, I would be willing to bet that you have more than enough money to make you happy. It is the chasing of financial success that often leads to misery in most, or all, of the above categories. **If you are chasing financial success in hopes of finding happiness, know that you would be the first person in human history to find it— if you ever reached that ever-moving target.** Without redefining success, you may never have a chance at achieving it.

The answer to your above definitions are going to be your new files. They will help you lay out the path to achieve your dreams. It is critical to come back to this list at least once a year to see if your definitions have changed. So often we are working toward a goal that we aren't even interested in anymore. We just forgot to re-assess and recalibrate for the correct target.

"Success without fulfillment is failure."
– TONY ROBBINS

REPUTATION

"A good reputation and respect are worth more than silver and gold."
– PROVERBS 22:1

There is a value for integrity I am going to share with you that only a person who has fully committed to a life of integrity can enjoy—an unquestionable reputation. If you commit 100 percent to integrity and live by these values and rules every day, your reputation will quickly be noticed and spread.

First of all, 99.999 percent of humanity either doesn't know what this even means or doesn't care for it, so you will instantly be part of a very small segment of the human race. This makes it easy for people to recognize, and they won't be able to help themselves but to talk about you in a positive light. Plus, **the longer you stay in integrity and follow this lifestyle, the more exponential the spread of your reputation will be.**

One of my favorite things about having a reputation of being a man of integrity is how many people share with me that I have inspired them to work on their own. This is beautiful, because that focus on integrity will most certainly change how they treat others, impact every relationship in their lives, and truly change the planet for the better. Is that not something you would be interested in doing?

Next, think of how valuable this is for our children. I would hate for you to read this section and think that I'm bragging, but I struggle to find another way to tell you all the benefits to your reputation without using my personal stories. So please offer me some mercy. I rarely go a month without someone coming up to me, while I am with my family, to shake my hand and tell me how I have positively impacted their lives. My kids get to constantly be reminded that living life the way I am teaching and showing them will in fact change many lives all around them. I pray you get to experience that feeling of being complimented, encouraged, and affirmed in front of your children for living this lifestyle. If you commit to it, this will happen for you.

But this isn't just about fun moments with the family or feeding your ego, this is about business and relationships and positively impacting the world. **In business, your reputation will precede you, and it will change how business dealings are offered and done. Better opportunities will be presented to you. Better business partners will approach you. Better offers will be made because your reputation carries its own hefty value and being associated with you now changes the value you offer.** It will be more critical than ever to stay focused on integrity to discern which opportunities are best for you long-term, which businesses you want to be associated with, and what you want your legacy to be.

In relationships, your integrity creates benefits of immeasurable value. Have you met many wives that regularly encourage their husbands to go on golf trips, to buy that incredible sports car, or to have an extra drink and enjoy himself? Mine does! Yes, that absolutely has to do with how awesome Brooke is more than anything else, but a small contributor is the fact that she knows I am a man of integrity and I will never break her trust. She knows with perfect certainty I will never lie to her and that I would never put myself in a compromising position, so she can be perfectly confident in our love no matter where I am or what I am doing.

Committing to this 100 percent integrity lifestyle will bring you endless benefits and a life of peace. It will take time for people to recognize the changes in you, and it will take even longer for your reputation to spread. Remember that these are simply extra benefits; I only share them to encourage you and to help you further solidify your commitment to living this way.

Fun Story

This is a silly one, but a family favorite in the Kaulius home! One day while shopping at Costco with my family, a young Costco employee came running over to tell me and my family the impact I have had on his life. We enjoyed the moment together, took a couple of photos, and were on our way. The very next day, while driving with my family, a car pulled up next to us and started honking to get our attention. The driver held up a bottle of Magnum DNA (a great product we make at Magnum), gave a big flex, and yelled, "I'm a huge fan!" We all laughed and waved and flexed back at him. My kids tell that story all the time.

LIVING WITH YOURSELF

One final thought I'd like to share about integrity is this: you will be alone with your thoughts for your whole life, so it is imperative that you like who you are! Living a life of integrity will keep you aligned with who you want to be, and will make you a human who enjoys their own company. Because you will be with yourself ten thousand times the amount of time anyone else will be with you, make sure you like yourself before you spend too much time caring about what others think. Living a life with integrity, a life in alignment, will positively impact so many areas of your life. Without it, it will be hard for the other principles in this book to make any impact at all. Finding your integrity and dedicating your life to it is step one in becoming the high-achieving world leader I know you can be.

CHOICE

No matter what situation you find yourself in, how you see the situation and, inevitably, how the situation concludes, are choices you make. Please read that again carefully so you don't misunderstand what I am saying. I am not saying you chose to be in the situation you are in; I am saying you have the choice of where you go from here.

As we discussed previously, our lives are made of stories we tell ourselves. Any given fact can be looked at in thousands of ways, depending on how you want to tell the story. A man can be forever sad about the girl who broke his heart, or he can recognize that getting dumped opened his eyes to how he could do more with his life. Getting his heart broken was actually the best thing to happen to him.

We all know someone who has lost their job. One can look at that as devastating and fall into sadness and depression, or one can see it as an opportunity to upgrade (by the way, almost every person in my circle needed to lose their job to become the unicorn they are today; losing the job was the best thing to happen to them). We have a million choices per day about how we want to view our circumstances.

Inevitably, someone will want to bring up illness. Again, I do not suggest anyone chose to fall ill (other than colds—colds are a choice; I will share that with you later in this chapter). But how you view illness and what you do about it is a choice. If, God forbid, you get the diagnosis of a serious illness, no one will blame you for immense sadness. But the people who choose to live bigger through the illness are always the best stories! Everyone feels uplifted hearing about the patient with an incredible attitude (regardless of the outcome). **We have the choice to become statistics or great leaders.** I know which one you have chosen to be.

What about trauma? No, I am not even slightly suggesting that anyone chose to go through their trauma—but I am suggesting that they can choose what to do about it. Just as with a bad diagnosis, no one would ever blame someone with difficult trauma in their life for shutting down. I wish it on no one. What happened is fact, and no one is calling that into question. What isn't set in stone is where you go from here. **You have the choice to focus on the past or focus on the future. If you went through trauma, know that your story could inspire and strengthen millions.** You have an opportunity most do not—you have the chance to reach others who also went through something. If you have found a way to turn it into your superpower, you will change lives every day. That choice is yours to make—will you be a victim or a champion?

"Pain is inevitable, suffering is optional."
– BUDDHIST PROVERB

One of the most incredible, inspirational men I know was born with Oromandibular Limb Hypogenesis Syndrome—he was born with no legs and one partial arm. Nick Santonastasso did not choose to be born like this, but he has a choice every day to take the hand he was dealt and play the hell out of it. Because Nick chooses to view his story as something incredible, he tours the world with Tony Robbins and inspires millions of people.

My inspiring friends, Duane "The Rock" Johnson (left) and Nick Santonastasso, epitomize the importance of choosing to stay positive.

I asked Nick how he views choice when it comes to living his inspiring life. Because his answer was so beautiful and full of wisdom, I present parts of it here virtually unedited from our conversation (with his permission, of course):

Most people focus on what they don't have versus what they have, and when you focus on what you don't have you start to put yourself in an unresourceful state. A state where you can't think about solutions, you're not optimistic, you can't see a compelling vision because you're always focused on what looks wrong.

Now, the other pattern is **focusing on what I can control versus what I can't control.** There are a lot of things you can't control and will bring a lot of uncertainty in your life. People are talking about recession and winter and it's a tough time, and there's two different types of people: there's one person who lets the external world dictate your internal world and there's one person who focuses on their internal world and they build armor to the external world. Oftentimes as well, **people think that the external world is going to fix the internal world, but nothing you ever get in the external world is going to fix the internal world.** Business and life are a spiritual game— an internal game. The last thing you choose to focus on in an internal game is the past, present, or the future.

The only time that you should be focused on the past is finding the gifts. Finding the gifts and finding the lessons. You can choose to focus on the present moment, which is where all the gold is, but oftentimes the people that you're speaking to, they're action takers and achievers, they love to focus on the future. You and I love to focus on the future, the things that we're going to build and create.

The other thing when it comes to choice that gets my brain going is you choose the meaning you give things. Meaning equals emotion and emotion equals life.

What is the meaning that you're giving things?

Is this a problem in my life or is this a worthy opponent that will call me to do more, to give more, to serve more, to impact more?

So, when it comes to choice, just to tie it all in a bow, you need to make a decision to change your life. **It all comes down to a decision.** When you decide, you commit, you burn the boats, but a choice is: I choose what I focus on, I choose the meaning that I give things in my life, and I also say that I choose that I find the gift or I find the problem. **The problem is always there if you want it, but the gift is always there if you want it too**; most people just aren't ready to find the gift. They want to sit in the diaper, they want to sit in the poop, and they want to stay in that victim mentality rather than finding the gift and forcing themselves to find the learnings so they can get out of that victim mentality.

– NICK SANTONASTASSO

CHALLENGE

You might find this challenge a little messed up and dark, but I promise you I have been doing this for decades and have found great success with it. I take whatever problems I am faced with, or the trauma I am dealing with, and I picture myself explaining to someone like Nick how rough I have it. Take the time to really visualize sitting down with Nick and explaining why you have it so hard and how he wouldn't understand. I have always found this works wonders for me in putting my problems into perspective and turning my story more positive.

This is not an exercise to teach you that your problems are insignificant. What you went through or are going through is real and no one is taking that away from you. But you have a choice right now to sit down and stop moving forward because of it or to use it as a fire to propel you forward. The point of mentally sitting down with my boy Nick is to see him telling you that what you went through doesn't have to define you or end your story—it can be the beginning of one of the greatest stories ever told.

YOU CAN HAVE EXCUSES OR RESULTS, BUT YOU CAN'T HAVE BOTH

I don't care how cliché that title is; it is 100 percent true. I love calling myself and my clients on excuses. **We live in a society that encourages laziness and excuses.** This world relies heavily on all of us believing "you deserve that extra hamburger today," and "binging that show on Netflix for six hours straight is totally okay, you work hard!" It feels like in every way, marketers are looking for us to settle and be complacent. That doesn't sit well with me.

As you go through the challenges below, I hope you discover that excuses are in direct competition with results. **Every excuse you accept takes you further from your goals.** Recognizing what an excuse looks like (as it comes in many forms) is going to be a critical first step in overcoming them. The more you recognize them, the closer you will come to seeing and hearing excuses almost constantly throughout the day.

Start with asking yourself this question: Why did I not accomplish all I wanted to today? I am confident that any answer you give (other than "I did") will be some form of an excuse. I am not saying your excuse wasn't incredible or didn't deserve your attention, but it is either an excuse or you achieved the results you were trying to achieve.

Here are a few industries that rely 100 percent on you accepting your excuses over your goals:

- Alcohol
- Tobacco
- Drugs
- Social media
- Fast food
- Streaming services
- Pharmaceuticals
- Pornography

Quite the list, eh? If you had to decide if that list represents the "good guys" or the "villains" in the human experience, which would it be? I am not saying there is never a place for a cocktail, and I am certainly not saying streaming services don't entertain, and yes some people need their meds—but how many people have taken these things and allowed them way too much space in their lives? Once you remove the veil, you can take control and decide for yourself how much of a role these excuse creators will play in your life.

CHALLENGE

For the next forty-eight hours, I want you to write down every time you use an excuse for yourself. You will need to be sharp and focused all day to catch yourself because, just like the white lies we discussed earlier, our lives have been built with excuses baked right in. Most people are appalled by the volume of excuses we give ourselves.

ADVANCED CHALLENGE

Take the above list and write beside each excuse what you could have achieved had you not accepted it. Example:

I deserve to sleep in today vs. I could have got my workout in

Fast food is easier and more convenient vs. I could have been a step closer to my ideal physique

I need these three hours of TV time vs. I could have read six chapters in this book

I love this exercise because you now clearly see the consequences of excuses. I hope you recognize the negative impact they play in your life and work every day to shut future excuses down and live the life of integrity I know you want to live. **Take back the control.**

This principle is closely tied to ownership. I am a huge fan of the book *Extreme Ownership* by Jocko Willink and Leif Babin. The book explains that if you want to accomplish all that you want to accomplish, you must accept that you are in full control and you must take ownership of the outcome. I will give you an extremely condensed summary, but I highly encourage you to read the book.

Whatever the results, if you take extreme ownership you accept that you had control over the outcome.

Example 1: you were late for work. You can blame traffic and your alarm, but YOU are the one who could have set another alarm, woken up earlier, planned a better route, etc.

Example 2: you got a cold. You can blame your stress, your work, the cold weather, but YOU are the one who didn't deal with your stress better, you chose what work you would do, you could have worn more layers, you could have made sleep a priority, you could have taken more vitamins!

The point of this section is not to assign blame or make you feel guilty. But if you blame outside forces, there is no lesson to learn and history will almost certainly repeat itself. If you take ownership of the outcomes in your life, you will make the changes necessary to yield different, better results for your life.

"Good leaders don't make excuses. Instead, they figure out a way to get it done."
– JOCKO WILLINK

Fun Story

Covid started off as the scariest experience I have ever had in business. It was two days before fifty of my top athletes, my staff, and I were to fly down to Columbus, Ohio, for the Arnold Classic (Arnold Schwarzenegger's massive trade show). The show was abruptly canceled—a clear sign this Covid thing was about to wreak havoc on the world. It stunk that my company had invested over $200,000 into that show and stood to lose it all, but I knew it was only the beginning.

Since no one knew what this virus really was, the world stood still. People weren't spending money because no one knew if we were in a Matt Damon, end-of-the-world situation. My sports nutrition company saw a 70 percent decrease in sales that month and the next. There are no businesses prepared to drop 70 percent in sales. It was a horrifying experience. For the first time ever, I thought that my business might be taken away from me. As did many business owners, I threw myself a pity party.

After a few weeks, I woke up one morning and asked myself if I was enjoying the pity party. I remember saying to myself, "Someone is going to do very well during Covid. Many businesspeople will thrive." I instantly remembered that I am not a benchwarmer and I am that businessman who will thrive. I took a good, long look at myself, recognized my excuses, and got to work.

I came to the office that day, called in my executive team, and told them the moping around was over and from that day on, we would thrive. Since we had just recently moved into a huge new building (yes, that was extra stressful too, because the mortgage payment was more than double what it had been), I told the team to start thinking outside the box, like maybe getting some rental income from the extra space. As I saw faces and eyes fall (they couldn't imagine who would be wanting space at that moment) I reminded them that many businesses were killing it.

"You don't think companies making toilet paper and hand sanitizer desperately need space right now?" I reminded them that there were many businesses still growing, and that someone needed space—today.

The very next day (no exaggeration), we had a contract signed to take in 150 pallets from a company who made probiotic gum. The rent on this one contract was over $7,000 per month. **The energy in the building turned immediately. The fear was exiting.**

We had every right to use the excuse that Covid was killing our business. Everyone would have accepted it, including the bank as they seized my building and all my assets. Instead, I chose results, and the business became more streamlined, disciplined, and truly stronger than it had ever been before. In 2021 we broke our sales record.

IF IT'S NOT IN YOUR CONTROL, IT DESERVES ZERO MENTAL BANDWIDTH

I will warn you in advance, this is the section that will cause inner turmoil and resistance with many of you. Yes, I am about to trigger 50 percent of you. I am going to challenge you on how you spend your mental energy and time. Please know this before you read on: there is no judgment coming from me regarding how you spend your mental time and energy. That said, it is very rare to find ultra-successful people who don't spend their time thinking and talking the way I am about to describe.

The happiest, most driven people I know almost exclusively speak about things in their control. They talk about their businesses, their travel, their goals, their relationships, and the like. These topics of discussion empower them and inspire those around them.

I have always found the unhappiest people often choose to speak about all the things out of their control. They discuss politics, news, gossip, social media . . . The time you spend thinking and talking about these sorts of things (things out of your control) is time you are consciously dedicating to feeling out of control and powerless. Why do we ever choose to wash ourselves in feelings of powerlessness and sadness?

You might be someone who loves talking and thinking about these things. I ask you to grant me one last challenge before you shut me out of your life forever! Try a forty-eight-hour cleanse. For forty-eight hours, you will not turn on social media, the news, or anything political. You will also refrain from conversations about these things and about gossip. Now if I know you correctly, and I am confident I do, you have surrounded yourself with people who also love these topics, so I am going to help you script what to say to avoid them for forty-eight hours. When the topic comes up, you will politely say, "Do you mind if we avoid that topic tonight? I am trying to do a forty-eight-hour cleanse of politics, news, social media, and gossip." If the person you say that to cares about you in the slightest, they will support and encourage you on this cleanse and they will inquire as to why. What a great opportunity to start a new, positive dialogue.

After these forty-eight hours, what do you notice about your mood? Almost without fail, the answers will be: **I feel lighter. I have more energy later in the day. I sleep better. The world looked brighter today.** The weight and burden we carry by focusing on things out of our control make this life bleaker. Of course you barely have the energy to make it until 3 p.m. How do you expect to get ahead in life if you can't even keep up with the life you have right now?

I have lived the last twenty-five years of my life with almost zero news, politics, and gossip. Social media is a tough double-edged sword for a businessman, but I have managed to cut it down to under two hours per week. I give this discipline major credit for me being a happy human. You might think I am not in the know, and the world is passing me by without me knowing what is happening. Let me assure you, world news is all around us. You will still know what is happening in Russia and what the government has stolen from you today, but you will also have ten to twenty extra hours per week that you can now devote to positive things that will enhance your life, instead of negative discussions that only drain your life force.

I like to think of my brain much like a computer. If I open a whole bunch of tabs and have strenuous programs running at all times (thinking and worrying about my life, my work, the government, taxes, food, etc.), my computer will be slow and unproductive. I like to close tabs completely on the things out of my control; I try to open only one or two tabs at a time, put in the work on those applications, then close them down and move on. When I am in the gym, I am fully in the gym with no distractions. I don't check my phone, I don't answer texts or emails, I don't chitchat—I just get the gym job done. When I am with my kids or my wife, I like to be present and focus on them. I turn off the TV, I put down the phone, and I give them my full attention. If you try to do twenty things all at once, you will do half of them mediocrely at best and the others won't be touched (I hope the latter doesn't include your spouse!). **Be intentional with your time and your brain's bandwidth.** Protect it and use it only where you want to use it—it is the scarcest resource in your possession.

CHALLENGE

For the next forty-eight hours (yes, only two days), I would like you to go on a full Mind Diet (actually, more of a Mind Fast). I want you to cleanse yourself of all social media, gossip, and news. I am so excited for you. The next forty-eight hours will feel so freeing!

To properly cleanse yourself, you must be mentally prepared to avoid all social media, gossip, and news. Social media and news should be simple—just don't open the apps, and if someone sends you a link to anything on social media or news related, you are not going to open it until your fast is over (or maybe never if you love how it feels to be free of it).

Gossip will likely be the trickiest, especially because we all have so much gossip built into our lives that it isn't always easy to recognize it at first. You can come up with your own plan on how to avoid it, but my recommendation is simply to run! As you notice conversation turning to gossip, abruptly speak up that you are sorry, but you need to run. You may fill in the reason, just remember to keep it honest! "I just remembered somewhere I must get to" is perfectly honest since you did just remember that you are supposed to get away from that conversation and get to anywhere but there!

I will also encourage you to be prepared to fill the extra hours you now have in your days with something positive, like reading. If you don't have a plan for filling in the extra hours, you are far more likely to revert back to your default, which is all this bad stuff. Replacing such big life-drainers with something positive and life-giving will enhance your good feelings and motivate you to stay on this better path for life.

ADVANCED CHALLENGE

I am confident the first forty-eight hours on this Mind Diet has resulted in you being less anxious, having more energy for the day, feeling more optimistic about life, sleeping better, feeling an increase in your libido, being more patient with others, and so

many other wonderful benefits. Your advanced challenge is to continue for the full week.

Since you have already experienced benefits in only two days, imagine how seven days will feel. Is it really necessary to ever put these things back into your life? After the week is complete, you can decide how much social media and news you can handle in your normal life, but I encourage you to stay clean of gossip. Gossip will only bring negative feelings into your life and will hold you down. Gossip is also a form of lying (as you are unlikely speaking that way to the face of whomever the discussion is about) and will make you feel bad since you aren't living in integrity.

Have you noticed that it seems like you might be the topic of gossip from that group you were once part of? Isn't it sad to realize you were always a topic of it the moment you left earshot of that group? As with every principle and exercise in this book, I am helping you recognize the things in your life that are serving you and those that are draining you.

How good did that week feel? How much more energetic and productive were you? Imagine if you stayed on this path for a month, a year, ten years. Imagine how much further you could get in life and, more importantly, how much more you would enjoy that life. Please take time to ponder this and let that sink in. It is your choice to have that amazing life or stick to the path of news, social media, and gossip.

HOW WILL YOU SPEND YOUR NEW MENTAL ENERGY?

"Thoughts are mental energy; they're the currency that you have
to attract what you desire. Learn to stop spending that currency on
thoughts you don't want."
– WAYNE DYER

If you successfully took part in the last challenge, you now have extra mental energy to spend in your day. While yes, there are still other things we can do to increase our energy (exercising, for example, is an excellent energy booster—we will discuss this in a later chapter), most of what we do are expenditures. **How you choose to spend your mental energy is a critical concept if you want to reach new levels of success in life.** Do you want to be known as someone who "spends" his time or "invests" his time?

In this section I am going to discuss other drainers we spend our mental energy on that bring zero value to our lives, and exercises you can do to weed those out. **The more we eliminate these mental energy-drainers, the more energy we have available for our goals, dreams, and ambitions. We have far more time to invest than we realize.**

The first mental energy drainer is the past. Do not feel bad if I am describing you; the vast majority of humans spend an enormous chunk of their daily mental energy locked in the past. We spend it thinking about choices we made, relationships of the past, traumas, what-ifs . . . all these ideas that imprison us in questioning if we are on the right path or if our lives could be better. What if I had gone that way? What if that had never happened to me? What if I had said yes?

These questions do nothing to serve us or improve our lives. They do not make us wiser, they do not make us more likely to recognize the next opportunity, and they do not improve our chances of success in any way. What they do is create a routine in which we always question our decisions, allow focus to be spent frivolously on thoughts of negative value, feel out of control, and hinder our growth and our future. So how do we break this vicious thought pattern?

The first step is to recognize and admit these thoughts are not serving you. We need to learn our lesson from the past and quickly move on. **For all the countless hours you have spent in the negative thoughts of the past, what have you gained?** If I was standing in front of you, could you explain the benefits of this massive expenditure (in a way that I would agree with)? If you can admit it isn't serving you, you are ready to gain back a ton of mental energy and control.

The next step is to create new routines for the times when these thoughts pop into your head (sadly, they won't just disappear by tomorrow). Know that you will have to be diligent. You have created and reinforced these routines for years, maybe decades, so it will take some time for your new routines to become your default routines. Be patient with yourself and focus on the benefits of making this change.

We are going to replace these old, negative, out-of-your-control thoughts with new, positive, in-your-control thoughts. I want you to create a list of ten to fifteen exceptional things about yourself. I'd like the list to include things you are most proud of in life. Don't filter these through being humble or worrying about sounding arrogant—neither of those words will play a role here. You could have on your list things like:

- I am a loving husband
- I am a nurturing mother
- I am a deadly pianist
- I am a great golfer
- I am passionate
- I care for those less fortunate

You can go in any direction you'd like with your list, as long as the list is positive and true! Now, any time the old thoughts pop up, I want you to stop the thought in its tracks and shove one of your list items in its face. I want you to take a moment to soak in these positive thoughts long enough to forget the others. Feel free to think about specific moments that prove this positive trait.

To make sure your positive list is at the forefront of your mind and always ready to spring into action at a moment's notice, I want you to write your list, one by one, on sticky notes and put them all around you. Anywhere you might need to be reminded of these awesome things about you—that's where the notes should be. Later in the book I will dive more into the value of sticky notes and how they will change your life!

CHALLENGE

For the next forty-eight hours, I want you to be on high alert and stop these thoughts in their tracks. Do whatever you need to do to recognize when those thoughts are popping up and replace them immediately. Communicate your goal to the people closest to you and ask if they would like to join in the challenge. I find having others do these challenges with me keeps me more accountable, and I love having someone there to call me on my misbehaviors. Helping others on their journey to self-improvement will also bring you a world of added benefits (there is a whole chapter on service later in the book).

ADVANCED CHALLENGE

I want you to go seventy-two hours consecutively without spending more than one minute at a time in your old thoughts. One minute is more than enough time to catch yourself and replace the negative thought with a positive thought. If it takes you more than one minute, your seventy-two-hour clock starts over. **Once you have gone seventy-two consecutive hours without these old thoughts, you are going to notice a real difference in your positivity, your mental energy, and your outlook on life.** Now you just need to keep it going!

FORGIVENESS

"Not forgiving someone is like drinking poison and waiting for them to die."
– This quote has been credited over the years to Nelson Mandela, Buddha, St. Augustine, and about a thousand others! I don't personally care who said it, I just love the truth in it.

We just spent time working on ridding yourself of energy-wasters and freeing up more mental energy to put toward your goals.

No energy zapper is as powerful as holding a grudge. At many points in my life, I refused to forgive someone who wronged me. I spent countless hours stewing over it and allowing those negative thoughts and emotions to fill my every cell. I remember holding on to so much anger toward someone that there was rarely a fifteen-minute slot in the day when their face didn't come into my thoughts. Can you relate? Think of how many days of productivity I lost to the choice I made to hold on to this poison.

You must find a way to forgive and let go of all the negativity and pain that comes with holding on. To start, reflect on the quote above, the one attributed to a thousand wise people. Recognize the truth in it—that your choice to hold on to that pain impacts you and you alone. To be clear, I am not saying you must now go to the person that wronged you and become best friends. Forgiving and forgetting are two different concepts. You can absolutely wish someone happiness and peace without spending time with them or pretending nothing happened.

The first step here is to recognize that your anger toward that person affects you only. Know that you carrying this pain doesn't negatively impact them even one bit. Step two requires strength and courage and the discovery of just how incredible you can be. You need to forgive them. How did I get through this challenging step? I prayed for my enemies.

If you are not a praying human, that's okay. Whether it be "putting it out there to the universe," or "making a wish," or whatever you normally do in lieu of prayer, do that. **Since I started the practice of praying for my enemies, I have been able to let all grudges go. It is very hard to keep hate in my heart for someone that I daily pray for and in full integrity hope will find happiness and fulfillment in life.**

I will be honest, this will likely not be an easy road in the beginning. You need to find truthful words that you can speak about wishing them well. For me, I pray that they find peace and joy in the Lord, and I honestly mean it. If the people I once wished ill toward were to find joy and peace in God, they would very likely recognize the roll they played in my past pain and apologize. They would likely also feel that pain and want to never hurt anyone else in that way again. Imagine how great the world would be if the people who hurt us truly felt the pain they caused and worked the rest of their days making sure no one else felt that pain from them. Isn't that the kind of planet you want to live on? Can you use that to utter well-wishes and the words of forgiveness?

I pray now that you can find your way to this path. It is remarkable how different your mind will work if you practice this daily. Not only do I find myself truly wishing my old enemies well, but I find myself feeling extra merciful toward them. Think of the pain in their lives that would lead them to treat someone the way they treated me. Imagine the lack of love they must have experienced in their lives. Imagine the pain they live in every day. With the mercy and pity I feel, how can I possibly hold hatred in there as well? And with that mercy and love replacing the hatred and anguish, I am free to absolutely dominate my life. My success will be the ultimate statement to show all those people that "they can't hurt me!"

Personal story: For almost three decades I held contempt and anger toward my father. I have brought up multiple times already the major role that growing up without him played in my life. I was so sad and angry that my father wasn't there for me when I was getting bullied, when I was learning about girls, when I needed guidance about being a man, when I was hurting, when I was celebrating, when I needed discipline, or when I needed someone to tell me he was proud of me. I carried this pain into every relationship I had, and I allowed it to taint my view of the world.

One blessed day, by God's grace, I finally allowed this principle, and so many other principles in this book that for whatever reason I hadn't allowed into this one sore spot, to change my story. I realized that **I became who I am because of the life I've had.** If I'd had a father who was there, I would certainly have turned out to be someone very different.

I was reminded of my relationship with my wife and what it was like when we were falling in love. Brooke loves and respects her father and they have an incredible relationship. When I first met Brian (and Heather, Brooke's mother), they could immediately see how broken I was, but that I had put my broken life in God's hands. As amazing Christian parents, they instantly showed me so much mercy and love. I had never experienced anything like this in my life, and I did everything I could to show them enormous respect and love in return.

If I had a father close to me in my life, it would have been very unlikely that I showed that level of love and respect for Brian. The love and respect I showed him came from decades of pain and desperation, longing for a father figure. I am nearly certain I would not have ended up with Brooke if I had a father in my life. She adored her father so much. If I hadn't come to her door with the love and respect for Brian that I did, I don't know that we would have ended up together.

If you asked me if I would flip the thirty years I considered pain by not having a father in my life if it meant I would be unlikely to end up with Brooke, I would say "No freakin' way!" My story led me to Brooke. My story made Brooke fall in love with me and give me over twenty years of love. My story now includes two beautiful daughters that I shower with the love I believe a father should shower their children with. As an added bonus, I got to receive extra love from Brooke's parents and got that void filled in my life too!

HOW COULD I NOT FORGIVE MY FATHER FOR THE ROLE HE PLAYED?

I am sad for him that he missed out on having a son like me and taking credit for all the good stuff in my life. I feel sad for him that he missed out on all the laughs and pats on the back every time I had a public achievement. I feel sad he doesn't get to know his grand-daughters: the two most amazing young women I have ever met. I am sad he didn't get to experience the loving, adoring son I was ready to be—I would have been my father's biggest cheerleader.

I am grateful for the father I had. Because of his absence, I became stronger. I am independent. I work my butt off. I know the value of a dollar. I encourage and reassure other young men who I can see the same fatherless brokenness in. Because of the pain I know it can cause a child to be without a father, I am there for my children 24/7—I owe that to my father as well. **My father had a major role in my life, and he played it perfectly.** How can I not appreciate him for that?

Does my story resonate with you? Do you see how a little change in your story can make a massive change to your life? Take time today to think about how your story can change like mine did. Can you tell a new story and change your perspective on your past?

Dad, I am sorry for all the years I placed blame on you and you bore the heat of my anger. You did what you were supposed to do, and I am who I am today because of you. Thank you, Dad. I forgive you and I hope your life is blessed beyond measure for all your days.

CONFIDENCE

Your confidence level is a choice. You can make that choice right now—just as I made the choice to be a more confident 120-pound, 6'4", fifteen-year-old boy, even though nothing had changed in my life but my mind. With the exercise we did in creating your new, more confident "character," you now have the choice to either bring that version of you into everyday life, or to stick with the character you've been playing up until now. **I have no doubt the current you is a wonderful person, but you wouldn't be reading this book if you didn't believe there was more to life than what you have experienced.** Let's continue to write your new story, starring a more confident you!

As with every other principle in this book, our main goal is to get these new principles to be your default ideals and routines. To make sure you are always bringing the more confident version of you into every situation, you will need to set constant reminders for yourself so it is always in your face to choose confidence. Set alarms in your phone to go off every hour that you are awake to "be the more confident you," write the same sticky notes in your bedroom, bathroom, car, wallet, desk, etc. These reminders should be so frequent that you can't do much without being reminded. Within a few weeks, I am confident we will have changed your default setting to the more confident you.

I want to remind you that confidence changes the way you do everything. Confidence changes the way you react to information, confrontation, misunderstandings, compliments, criticisms, handshakes, hugs, eye contact, driving, speaking, thinking . . . so remember to filter all of life through your new confident eyes. You will need to rewrite tons of old files. Remember to take note of how each of these situations feels different. Do you like the way they feel now? More than how they usually feel? Do you believe the results long-term will be better now or the old way?

As a fun mini-challenge, I'd like you to read the next three sections as the more confident you. How would the more confident you read, absorb, implement, and utilize these next principles and challenges? If you notice a difference in how it feels, how about getting into character before reading the remainder of the book?

YOUR BODY IS TALKING TO YOU, IT IS TIME TO LISTEN

Our bodies are one thousand times more user-friendly than we give them credit for. They send out clear messages when there is an issue, we just need to make sure we are listening. **If you do not listen to your body, your productivity, focus, strength, mindset, and chances of success can be brought down by up to 100 percent!**

Let's start with the most obvious signals—your body doesn't like the fuel you are putting in. Much like a car, your body has simple fueling requirements. Would you ever put a bottle of pop into your car's gas tank? What would happen if you did? Well just because some marketer told you that you can put that stuff into your body's fuel tank, it doesn't mean you should. **The same result happens if you put garbage in your gas tank or in your mouth; you're going to experience some malfunctioning.**

In the beginning you feel sluggish and lethargic, with possible short bursts of energy from the sugars. Already you are operating well under 100 percent. But as you continue to make poor dietary choices, the next level of malfunctioning occurs. For some, this will present with heartburn, indigestion, bowel issues, poor sleep, or erectile dysfunction, and others will start getting sick far more often, experience more aches and pains, headaches, soreness, etc. Sadly, our society (and the marketers) now tell you to get on a prescription to essentially shut your body up. How is that working out for us? If we only listened to our bodies, 99.9999 percent of us would not need prescriptions for indigestion, heartburn, high blood pressure, and many other ailments.

I want to pause to make a clear point about people who get really sick (cancers, heart issues, etc.)—I am NOT saying that they are at fault. Please don't misread and put those words in my mouth. But it is a medical fact that some of those people could have avoided that fate.

I decided long ago to listen to my body and look at food as a fuel source only. Our bodies can flourish and be incredible allies to us if we give the body what it was designed to work with: clean proteins, good carbs, essential fats, fruits, vegetables. No, this doesn't mean you will never see me with an ice cream cone or a piece of cake, but it does mean I watch how often I have those things and always on my terms (I have a treat meal 2–3 times per month).

I firmly believe that 100 percent of colds are a choice. Don't CHOOSE to get a cold! Our bodies send us clear signals when we are susceptible to a cold, but sadly, most of us choose to ignore those signals too. If you have a poor night's sleep, how do you feel the next day? Your body is likely screaming at you to take it easy. This is not the right time to skip meals, fuel yourself with garbage, stay out late, go out drinking, or to push yourself in any way. How often do we do exactly that? And what was the result? How was your productivity that day and the 2–7 days following? Next time you see those signals, choose to take it easy, eat right that day, get home as soon as possible, and get to bed early. That will be one slightly less productive day, but far more productive days will follow. This follows the over/under paradigm.

THE OVER/UNDER PARADIGM— WHEN TO MAKE DECISIONS

This is an incredible and simple mindset technique that my brother and I have been teaching for years and have seen radically change many people's lives. Over or under the line represents where your mental state is when you are making any decision. Being under means you are in a bad place: maybe you are having a terrible day, you got horrible sleep, you are in a major fight with your spouse, work has you stressed big time . . .

When you are "under"—much like being under water—your only concern should be to get yourself back to the surface to breathe normally. Wouldn't you agree that if you were drowning, that would be the worst possible time to make important decisions about your finances or your relationship?! While you are under the line, we suggest you don't make any decisions other than deciding to get back above it.

Under the line is where we experience resistance—we resist the situation we are in. "This can't be right. I can't believe this is happening. I don't deserve this." If we resist or deny our reality, we are unable to create solutions. Think of how quickly this line of thinking leads to resentment, and ultimately revenge—"I deserve better and need to right this wrong."

This is the state we are in when we spend time thinking about the past or negative situations in our lives. If we spend time thinking, "I can't get anywhere because my ex-wife ruined me" or "This government is boxing me in and won't let me grow," we are creating our own prison and reinforcing the locks because getting ahead would require us to prove ourselves wrong!

Get yourself to the surface (over the line), take a breath, and

calmly look at the decisions in front of you. To start, accept that "what is, is." Your ex-wife might have done some damage and the government is taxing you, but now what? Accept the reality and make some moves.

For clarity and comfort, know that acceptance is not the same as agreeing, approving, or condoning. You can accept that you are in a bank that is being held up without approving of the robbery.

Over the line is where you operate optimally. This is when you are thinking clearly, focused, centered, and in a great place to make decisions based on wisdom and good data. This is where you should be when making any decision.

Above the line is where you accept the situation you are in and are free to see your purpose and create. Recognizing the situation for what it is allows us to figure out what we are supposed to do, how to move forward, and where we are trying to go.

In all I have just written and in the examples I gave, you may have noticed that emotions are usually high when we are below the line. If you remove emotion and keep calm, you will often find yourself above the surface more quickly.

If you always think in terms of over or under the line and only make decisions when you're above it, think of how much better your choices and relationships will be. Your one and only focus when you are under the line is to get yourself back over. My brother and I like to ask each other, in those times when we see the other under the line, "How long do you want to spend under there?!"

My friend and mentor Tony Robbins refers to this principle as being in a positive or peak state:

Achieving your peak state requires letting go of the past, mastering your emotions and adopting a mindset of excellence. When you operate at peak state, you refuse to live a life of compromise or mediocrity. You operate at a higher level—and inspire others to do the same.

Our emotions are the foundation that peak state is built upon. They have the ability to control everything in our lives—our mood, our decisions and our actions. If you want to start making positive progress, you need to get into a positive state.[*]

FOUR BURNERS OF LIFE

The four burners of life is one of the greatest concepts about time and energy I have ever learned, and it truly changed the way I focus on any given task. The argument is that we have four focuses in our lives that you can picture like the four burners on a stove. These four burners represent family, health, friends, and career. You must decide where you want to route the power (your focus).

To start, all burners run at around 50 percent. I believe this is where most people leave them and find very little success in any of them. If you turn up one burner, it must come at the cost of another burner. If you try to have all burners on 100 percent, the argument is you will burn out and the whole system will collapse (I believe we have all witnessed people trying this). If you want to focus 100 percent on your career, it will come at a cost to your health, or family, or friends, or a little from each.

I will encourage you now to pause your reading for a moment

---

[*] Robbins, Tony. "Discover Your Peak State: How Emotional Triad Psychology Can Change Your Life." TonyRobbins.com/stories/unleash-the-power/discover-your-peak-state/.

and think about where you have routed your power and where you would like to route your power. The great news is you can change this focus at any time, and you will inevitably want to make changes at different stages in your life.

In my heaviest business growth days, I turned my career burner up to 100 and my health burner up to 90. This left both my family burner (I wasn't married at the time) and my friends burner at almost zero (I was a terrible friend, son, and brother). I have changed the orientation many times, and recently I have increased family and friends time at the cost of my career focus.

Whatever orientation you have chosen with your four burners, **I want you to fully commit to your decisions and not waste time and energy on regret.** Take your time with the decision and once you have made your choices, be unapologetic about how you spend your time.

I see many people choose a similar orientation to mine, then beat themselves up for not calling mom every week. If you are choosing to turn your family burner way down for a period of time, accept that mom gets that call once a month and don't burden yourself with guilt—that will only slow you down and weaken all burners.

As I am a huge fan of communication, I highly recommend discussing your burners with the people you care about. You can let mom or your friends know that you are going through a season where you need to focus on your career and you won't be around as much, but look forward to possibly reigniting that burner in the next chapter. **The lack of communication here is what hurts people, as they don't know why you aren't around as much.** By communicating it to them and explaining your why, you give them the opportunity to be part of the decision.

CHALLENGE

Take time now to choose how to orient your burners. Write it down. Mentally run through some scenarios to confirm you are able and willing to commit to this setting. Will it cause you to miss some family dinners? Will you be unavailable for some birthday parties? Are you okay to be single for a while? If you are ready, lock it in and stay committed. Be prepared to give yourself grace in lieu of guilt for turning down the burners that you turned down. Who will you need to communicate your choices to?

ADVANCED CHALLENGE

Set an alarm in your phone or computer to evaluate your choices in thirty days. How has it been going? Are you happy with your choices? Do any of the burners need to be tweaked? Are you remembering to not guilt yourself for your choices? If all is well, you can set your next alarm for sixty or ninety days and go through the same evaluation process. The timeline isn't as important as the practice of checking in and making sure your burners align with your goals and lifestyle.

Whatever you choose for your burner orientation, commit to it fully. Be intentional with your time and energy. Focus on the present, not the past. These are your decisions, so make your choices and go.

DROPPING YOUR VICE

With no judgment, we need to discuss pornography, drugs, and alcohol.

Without knowing it at the time, the first time I took a year off alcohol, I was building in myself a strength that could never be taken away. I believe I was twenty years old when I just didn't feel great about some of the decisions I was making while drinking. I heard a wise man once say "all the worst decisions I made in my life were under the influence of alcohol."

I decided to take a full 365 days off booze. Let me tell you right now, 100 percent is so much easier than 99 percent. Telling people you are off booze, doing a cleanse from booze, fasting from booze is far easier than saying "maybe not tonight." I think we all know that friends will see that opening as a challenge to try to break you!

I should mention that I didn't have a "problem" with alcohol. I was a casual drinker, maybe once a week or every two weeks, but often I drank to get drunk. I didn't see how this would serve me in my career goals or in my faith, so I took the challenge.

As you can imagine, the first month or so was tough. Seeing my friends having a great time in front of me, telling me stories of what happened after I went to bed at 10 p.m. (ever notice how things get boring by 9:30 without alcohol?), and always reminiscing about the last time we all drank together . . . this made me feel left out and a little incomplete, as I was no longer a key character in their stories. **But the benefits were immediate and only strengthened my resolve.**

Let's start with zero hangovers! Never missing a workout because I slept in, my body was getting tighter, my brain was functioning stronger, and I was no longer making really bad drunken decisions. Since drinking buddies aren't usually good for pushing each other to get ahead in life, I started surrounding myself with bigger thinkers. Big shock—great things started to happen.

In that year I went to Vegas with my guys twice! In heading down, I thought the no-drinking thing would be an issue, but it wasn't. I was more than happy to take part in all the things they wanted to do and I was still a good time. It's also always nice to have a sober "handler" with you to keep you out of trouble in Vegas, so they appreciated me more than ever.

It wasn't until I was older and wiser that I realized what I had really done by taking that year off alcohol—**I had created a clear, permanent rule that alcohol would have no control over my life.** At any point, I could drop it again (which I did, by the way—I took another year off a few years later, then I took five years off recently). I now realize I was also building a discipline that couldn't be taken from me. This discipline crosses over into every aspect of life—I can do (or not do) whatever I choose.

Does any of my history feel a little too relatable? Is it time to consider taking some time off alcohol yourself? If a year seems daunting, how about just one month to start?

I do need to state the obvious—it would be hard for anyone to argue that alcohol will help you in your quest for success. I don't mean to be a buzz kill, but at some point you should have a real discussion with yourself about how alcohol could ever help you in your journey.

To me, drugs and pornography fall into separate categories from alcohol. Let's start with pornography. I'm not going to jump into a lecture about how it will distort your ideas of sex and relationships; I am here to talk about how it will negatively impact your ability to succeed.

First question, how much time is it eating up of your day, your week, your month? How much further ahead in life would you be if you spent that time reading books, exercising, investing in yourself and your business? I shouldn't have to go any further than that, but I will anyway.

Vices on devices, such as pornography, gaming, and social media, have completely altered our brain functioning. Numerous studies have shown that this instant, repetitive, constant dumping of dopamine has brutally altered our ability to focus, our attention span, and our cravings for instant—and constant—gratification.

Not convinced? Try reading after your next session on a tablet or computer screen. How was your focus? How was your attention span and your ability to hold on to the knowledge? Now take twenty-four hours off devices and read again. See the difference? **If you want to experience great success in life (I said great, not tiny tastes of success), you will need to start catching and evaluating anything that has this sort of negative impact on your brain, your focus, your time, and your energy.**

How does pornography affect your relationships? If you answer honestly, you know that even if you are the 1 percent who doesn't hide it from their partner, you do not feel good about what you are doing and you know they don't (or wouldn't, if they knew) either. How can this massive secret possibly be considered healthy for your relationship? This goes back to inner congruency and integrity. To be a true leader and titan of industry, and to discover true happiness, you need to listen to that inner voice and stop doing the things that cause this kind of guilt, sadness, and regret.

And finally, drugs. Before we talk about how drugs are impacting your life, I would like to take a moment to shine light on the fact that there is no area in your life you can leave in the shadows if you want to experience real success and true happiness. There is no topic that shouldn't be discussed, no part of your life you shouldn't dissect to confirm it is in alignment with your goals.

How are drugs serving you? Now before you tell me that drugs and alcohol help you relax and give you a break from the harshness of reality, I'd like to suggest to you, as someone who has made it to "the other side," that **the harder you work toward your goals, and the more your life is in alignment with your potential, the less you will be interested in escaping your reality.** I think if you are being honest, you would say, "Of course drugs and alcohol aren't serving me." I'd like you to be honest right now, as that declaration is key to us moving forward.

I'd like to quickly remind you of all the ways these vices are blocking your road to success.

Time: Not only are you a write-off the night you partake, but for at least three days after, your brain isn't anywhere near max effectiveness. That's three days of less-than-perfect workouts, reading, focus, mental ability, studying, capitalizing . . .

Self-image: It is common for drug, alcohol, and porn users to indulge in self-loathing for what they have done—especially people who believe they are destined to do more with their lives. This self-loathing and battered self-image is extremely detrimental to your velocity toward success.

Money: That money spent on vices could have been spent on investments, and instead of taking you the wrong way, you could have been getting ahead.

If I have convinced you to take a break from your vices, but you are concerned about your ability to go cold turkey, the next section is about doing things in baby steps. We will get you through this.

Not-So-Fun Story

I would like to share with you my honest reason for taking five years off booze. I was hosting a golf tournament for my number one client—Popeye's Supplements Canada. Twenty-five of the owners (owning 120+ retail locations across Canada) were here in Vancouver, British Columbia, to golf with me and my staff. This group represented close to 60 percent of the sales of my business at that time. We had designed an incredible day that included ten of my local athletes out on the course laughing it up, pouring drinks, and making sure everyone was having a blast. I made sure I passed on many rounds of booze to keep my wits about me, but around hole 16, I started to let loose. When we arrived at the clubhouse for dinner after the round, one of my team, who had over consumed, started acting out and speaking aggressively—directed at our number one client!

Fortunately for me, this story didn't end in disaster. Just witnessing one of my team acting this way (I sent him home immediately to avoid a major issue) made me realize that booze could have crippled my business that day. What if I had acted out that way and no one was there to send *me* home? What if I had told off the wrong person and permanently harmed this relationship? I remember thinking in that moment, with such clarity, that I would never have had to worry about these things if alcohol was not involved. Why would I knowingly throw a tiger in a room and hope that no one dies?

Yes, there is a huge difference in having a drink or two versus getting drunk. Yes, I could have simply limited my consumption to always stay in that safe zone. But I decided that day that I would rather be known as the reliable, trustworthy, focused, always-working businessman than the guy who we sometimes party with and whom you can "usually" trust!

BABY STEPS TO MAKE MASSIVE CHANGE

We all want massive change in our lives, but how often do we find ourselves trying to take a huge leap only to fail when we recognize we have bitten off more than we can chew? I will use the analogy of the diet, as most people have failed on their diet at some point in their lives.

You have made the decision to lose weight. It is time to make change. Since you want results right now, you decide to do a full overhaul: five days training per week (from zero days per week), no more sugar (instead of all the sugar), no more alcohol . . . sound familiar? Is it really shocking when this hard plunge fails in under a month?

These changes are so big they aren't sustainable.

Now what if I asked you to start working out two times per week, replace two fast food meals per week with healthy foods, and to drink one less time this week? Doesn't that seem manageable? It isn't a drastic change to your life, and your body and mind won't be fighting you.

After two to three weeks, how about increasing it to three workouts per week, two less fast food meals again, and one less night of alcohol?

These baby steps are small, manageable changes that your body and mind can accept. They don't feel like someone has gutted your house and asked you to figure out the renovation for yourself. This will yield long-term, real change, and the baby steps concept can be applied to pretty much every aspect of life.

No matter what you are attempting to add or delete from your life, baby steps will increase your chances of success.

I have failed many times in my life to become a reader. When I realized I hadn't picked up a book in weeks, I would "commit" to reading at least an hour each day, every day. Day one and sometimes day two were okay, but then it fell apart. Worse than not sticking with the unrealistic goal I set, I was now speaking negatively to myself about failing again and what an undisciplined fool I had become.

How did I think that negative talk was going to improve the situation for me? The story I was telling myself was so harmful, and I naturally made that story true because it was easier to be that lazy, unread guy than to put an hour in every day. It was time to change my story.

When I applied baby steps to reading, I aimed to read just five pages each day. Five pages was perfectly manageable. I could get that done in under ten minutes. I often found myself sitting and reading for 30–60 minutes, absolutely destroying my goals and making me feel like a champion. And on the days I could only get my five pages done, I was still super happy with my achievement: I hit my daily goal. It wasn't long before I asked for ten pages, then twenty . . . and now I am always hungry for more reading, more knowledge, more growth. What a beautiful change from the guy who went two days strong, then bashed himself for his lack of commitment.

Take a moment to think about how baby steps can be applied to any area of your life. Do you want to be a better parent? Instead of attempting an extra hour every day with your kids, how about we start with ten minutes of uninterrupted time with them? **If you are looking to be a better spouse, friend, basketball player, French speaker, rock climber . . . you name it, baby steps will set you on a path for greater likelihood of success.**

CHALLENGE

Let's apply baby steps to the last section on vices. This week, I challenge you to cut down your vices by 20 percent. If you hit them five times per week, you only need to cut out one day. Manageable, right? In two weeks, I'd like another 20 percent reduction. Continue reducing at this rate until you are fully off your vice or have found a balance with your vice that you are truly aligned with.

ADVANCED CHALLENGE

Replace that vice time with something positive. "The three hours I would normally spend drinking tonight, I will read!" Think of how much further ahead you will be in a year with just this one little change!

Please tag us with #playabiggergame on social media and allow our community to surround you with support and encouragement. We are in this together and want to lift each other up. You should also look at other posts with that hashtag and lend out some encouragement and support to others on their journey as well.

THE A-ROD PRINCIPLE

This is one of my favorite principles, one that I have always lived by, but I only recently created structure for it. Since the structure came from a unique and fun story, I am going to build this principle with you as I share the tale of that fateful day.

I had an 8:00 a.m. flight booked from Vancouver to Los Angeles. Before going to bed the night before, I was well aware of the blizzard that was moving in and would likely wreak havoc on my plans. I was going to be having dinner at my friend Alex's house at 6:00 p.m., so I was hoping I had enough time, even if there were delays. I wanted to show up in a perfect, peak state when I got to dinner, so I committed to staying in that state, no matter what the weather threw at me.

This would be a little extra challenging. I had, sadly, made it a habit to feel some frustration if my travel plans didn't run perfectly. **But I knew that if I could just ONE TIME get through it and keep a smile on my face, I would set a new standard for all my future travel.**

I left the house around 5 a.m. to slowly get through the winter wonderland that made the twenty-five-minute drive to the Vancouver airport a solid ninety minutes. Miraculously, the flight was not delayed to load . . . but then the cold took over! We started with a forty-five-minute de-icing of the plane, followed by thirty minutes on the runway, hoping the snow would let up enough for us to quickly escape. No such luck. The captain came on to let us know that we were heading back to the gate to refuel.

"If we are allowed, we will try again!" he said.

I checked in with myself and made sure I was still in peak state, and I was! I reminded myself that it was a miracle to even be on a plane right now (they could have canceled it). I reminded myself that less than twenty-four months ago I wasn't allowed to fly anywhere (because of Covid). I reminded myself that I was off to a beautiful place, I had lots of healthy food on me to get me through, I had books to read and an entertainment system to abuse. I was calmly and privately smiling away as other passengers were cursing and complaining.

After ninety minutes at the gate, we pushed back to get in line for de-icing.

"Don't worry folks, there are only eight planes in front of us in line," the captain reassured us. He also let us know that he would do what he could—but he couldn't promise we were going anywhere that day.

Each plane took close to thirty minutes to de-ice. It had been over six hours since I had boarded the plane, and I was more energetic and full of joy than when I first stepped on. Then, we actually took off!

Twelve full hours after I left my house, I landed in LA. I stripped down in the LAX bathroom, shaved, took a shower in the sink, and got dressed to impress. I showed up in peak state and made memories that night that I will keep forever. You may know Alex by the name A-Rod.

The A-Rod Principle is a way to focus and give yourself a reason to set a new standard and tell a new story. I could have easily fallen in line with every other passenger and been pissed off about how the day went. I don't think Alex would have blamed me for showing up and complaining about the ridiculous day I had. But that would have been a very different dinner, I would have left a very different impression, and, in my opinion, our future relationship would not exist.

Just like we discussed at the beginning of the book when we talked about the four-minute mile, **until we do something once, our brains don't necessarily believe it is possible.** However, in proving it can be done, it opens up a world of possibility. Keeping this great attitude and perfect state during that crazy journey showed me that I CAN do it whenever I want to. I immediately thought back on some of the rough flights I'd had with my family and how my complaining made the trip sour. I forgave myself, but decided I would never allow that to happen again. I proved what was possible and I can't wait for the opportunity to show my family the man I am now. (Yes, I recognize I just wished for a flight delay in my future plans.)

Key Elements to the A-Rod Principle:

- **Commit to the result you want ahead of time:** "I will show up to dinner in my perfect state."
- **Plan and prepare to keep you on track:** You know what triggers you and what might derail you. I had enough food and books to keep me happy for days. Had I not brought the food, I would have lost my mind in the second hour! I also knew and accepted that the snow would delay things, so I planned to laugh off every delay.
- **Know what tools you have at your disposal in case you start veering off plan:** I had breathing exercises, stretches, prayer, and gratitude meditations if I needed to "remove myself" from the situation. I knew that just changing my physiology (standing up, stretching, walking a bit) could dramatically change my attitude and state.
- **Check in regularly on the journey to catch yourself early if you veer off course:** I asked myself how I was doing and made sure I was still smiling and exuding positive energy.
- **Celebrate the wins:** I was so happy with my results and knew I had an amazing story to tell. I was also so excited to share the story and the experience with my family. Plus they get a better version of me on our next trips! And I certainly celebrated the outcome—showing up to Alex's house in a perfect state and being part of a beautiful night.

Are there things in your life (attitudes, forgiveness, diet, exercise, vices) that you may subconsciously think are impossible to change? I am confident that you have already come across a few tricky subjects in this book that you have been hesitant to try to tackle. **This A-Rod Principle can show you what you are truly capable of.** You need to accomplish something just one time to set a new standard and show yourself that it isn't impossible. One workout, one clean meal, one day, one kind word can open up your mind and set you on a new course for life. Watch for your opportunity to exercise the A-Rod Principle this week.

WHEN SHOULD I GO FULL-TIME WITH MY SIDE HUSTLE?

The baby steps are over and it might be time to jump in the deep end. This has always been one of my favorite opportunities to work through with entrepreneurs. Because there are so many variables involved when plotting out a plan here, you will need to decipher what information best pertains to your story and how to apply it. I will give you multiple ways to look at this question, but your opportunity will have unique variables and challenges that will require you to think outside the box and adapt the process. Keep in mind that some of the questions below encompass many issues (like if your industry is growing or shrinking—this will greatly effect your likelihood of success).

- **Question 1:** If you made this your full-time gig, how much growth would you expect in the next six months, one year, three years?
- **Question 2:** Is this growth far higher than the growth expected if you did not go full-time with it (i.e., if you kept it as a side hustle)?
- **Question 3:** When can you expect to cover your living expenses from the income of going full-time?
- **Question 4:** Will going full-time with your side hustle bring

more joy to your life? (Take some time on this one. It might surprise you.)

- **Question 5:** What is the likelihood going full-time will bring you the wealth and lifestyle you are dreaming of? Or could it lead you to other opportunities that will make your financial dreams come true?
- **Question 6:** If things don't go as well as you hope, how long will your finances last? (If you are counting on your side hustle to blow up in thirty days or you and your family are out on the street, this is not likely the right time to jump! Keep it as a side hustle a while longer.)
- **Question 7:** Is there other important information to consider? Again, is the industry growing or declining? Is the space too crowded already or will you be able to carve out enough business?

Here is how my story unfolded as I asked these questions:

My bedroom supplement business was making me around $4,000 in profit per month (which felt awesome since it wasn't taking up more than ten hours per week). I had six guys working under me, doing the same business out of their bedrooms (what a bizarre franchise I had started). So I asked myself the big questions about my future with this business.

If I went at it full-time, I would need to train at different gyms and start being a little more aggressive than I was comfortable with in acquiring new business. To put in all those extra hours, it would be all about getting my name out there. The growth would come, but I felt it would come at a slow rate since this was no longer "organic growth"—I was going outside of my circles and the people who knew me. So I expected to put in significant effort for small additional gains.

To cover the income I was making as a server (shout-out, Earl's Restaurant) I was thinking it would take at least six to twelve months, but when I thought about hitting the $10,000 per month goal I had for myself, I just couldn't see it happening with this business, no matter how much hustle I put into it. I also recognized there was an inverse relationship between the extra work and joy. The more work I put in (which meant aggressively putting my name and cards out there with strangers), the less I was enjoying that work and the more I was also increasing my risk. (Remember, these are strangers coming into my bedroom and seeing the lack of security protecting tens of thousands of dollars in supplements . . . that weren't even insured!)

What an incredible exercise for me to follow. It was at this moment that I knew I had to make a serious pivot in my business. I started watching for other ways I could grow the business, and within three months I had my first storefront. Owning a retail location was nothing I had even thought of before, but in asking these big questions, having a retail location quieted all my concerns and put me on a path to reach my income, growth, and fulfillment goals.

Within twenty-four months I had my second and third locations. Once the first store was doing very well, I naïvely believed I could simply replicate the results and multiply the profits by three. O young Markus! How sweet and innocent you were!

While the volume of supplements I was moving through my stores was incredible, the challenges I was experiencing multiplied by ten. Staffing, theft, supply, support . . . this was the first time I truly learned "you don't know what you don't know."

So on January 17, 2005, I went back to my big seven questions, open to discovering what direction I should go next. I discovered that retail was not where I wanted to be. I had struggled to support many of the brands in my stores, as they didn't stand for integrity. I felt God blessing me with the incredible answer: you are going to have your own brand. It was that very day that Magnum Nutraceuticals was born.

Once again, asking these big seven questions opened my mind to possibilities. I could see that my current plethora of problems would only increase if I continued with more store locations. I recognized that if I had my own brand, I would build it with a foundation of integrity and filter every decision through that. Taking these steps would allow me to offer support to my store clients that I was unable to offer with other brands. And if I had my own brand, I could now solve the same problems for other supplement stores that were inevitably struggling with the same challenges I was. I instantly recognized that Magnum was my future.

Asking these questions became one of the greatest exercises I have ever done. The questions opened my mind and brought opportunities that I still can't believe came to me. In under three years, I made two major pivots and was put on a path that yielded 60 million times the success I was expecting!

Is there a version of these questions you can ask that pertains to your current employment? Getting your mind thinking about these things will open you up to great possibilities, and I hope one day you will share your amazing story of change with me. That story starts right now.

VULNERABILITY

Being vulnerable has taken on a completely new context in the last ten years. It was once seen as weakness. Today, being vulnerable is a beautiful thing that deepens relationships and creates relatability. Vulnerability is opening up and allowing others to see your inner workings—faults, weaknesses, and all. Being vulnerable draws people in. Being vulnerable requires courage and confidence.

It required vulnerability to admit that maybe I wasn't doing things perfectly in my bedroom supplements business. It was vulnerability that opened me up to changing my path and led me to incredible success. It is that same vulnerability that will always keep me open to learning, adapting, and evolving.

In business, being vulnerable helps keep your ego and pride in check. It was vulnerability that allowed me to ask the big questions about my business and accept that my business was not perfect. Vulnerability allowed me to ask people in my life that I admired what they saw as flaws in my business and if they saw things I didn't see.

The more I practice vulnerability with others, the more I discover new levels of connectivity, trust, intimacy, and success. As I open up and show vulnerability with my staff, admitting that I am not perfect and don't have all the answers, I witness them step up, learn, grow, engage, lead, and connect with me in ways I never experienced before. **Vulnerability is a key element in the culture I have built in many companies.**

"To love at all is to be vulnerable. Love anything, and your heart will certainly be wrung and possibly be broken. If you want to make sure of keeping it intact, you must give it to no one and nothing, not even an animal. You must carefully wrap it round with hobbies and little luxuries and routine and avoidances of entanglement, and then lock it up in the casket or coffin of your own selfishness. And this means that in the long run, the alternative to tragedy, or at least to the threat of tragedy, is damnation, for in that casket—safe, still, and unventilated in the darkness—it will go bad; not broken, but finally unbreakable, impenetrable, resistant to all good and joy."

– C. S. LEWIS

BE MINDFUL OF WHO IS IN YOUR CIRCLE

"You are the average of the five people you spend the most time with."

– JIM ROHN

I know you have heard this before, but it is imperative we dive into it to make sure you recognize the powerful role these five people play in your life. For whatever the characteristics you are trying to build up in yourself, your five will either lift you up or drag you down, depending on the strength of these characteristics in them. You must take the time to first recognize which characteristics you are looking to improve in yourself, then evaluate who will build you up and who will bring you down.

Let's discuss some of the character traits you might want to focus on (this is not an exclusive list—there will be many others you can add, and some of these will not be a focus for you).

- Ambition
- Consistency

- Faithfulness
- Discipline
- Vulnerability
- Enthusiasm
- Passion
- Mercy
- Forgiveness
- Health

If you are looking to be a remarkable human who accomplishes far more than the average, you must surround yourself with other high achievers. It has been my experience that this concept, and the resulting action that is required, is the greatest challenge and roadblock for most people and the reason why the majority ultimately choose to settle in right where they are. You can't be afraid to give space to those who are aiming at a very different goal than you and draw closer to those on the same path.

On paper, it seems like an easy task to move toward people with the same drive and focus as you, but **the role of comfort and false contentment impede most people's ability to make these tough choices.** If you aren't willing to do it for the "selfish" reason of wanting to get ahead in life, please do it to stop hurting your friends with less ambition! That's right, if you have high ambition and your friend doesn't, whether they are willing to admit it or not, you make them very uncomfortable.

Your drive and passion will always make them feel bad about their lack thereof. They would much prefer (again, whether they know it or not) to be surrounded by others with the same level of complacency for life. You make them feel bad. So, for both of you, your joy, and your level of desire for living, you need to give them space.

I would like to be very clear on this point: you do not have to kick these people out of your life. Yes, that is sometimes the answer, but the ultimate solution is to decide how much time you should be spending with each person. Some are undeserving of any of your time, some are deserving of a little, and some warrant tons! The important thing to understand and accept is that the decision is yours and that it has massive ramifications for your future.

Here's the exciting part: once you remove or minimize the time spent with the wrong people, you open up space in your life for the right people! Imagine the superstar just waiting on the bench, ready to be put into the game (your life). That superstar is ready to elevate your life in ways you can't even imagine, and you will play a major role in their success as well, but until you open up space for them and give them the opportunity to run, they can't make the impact on your life that they should.

Tony Robbins constantly stresses the importance of choosing the right people to spend time with. He encourages us to find people who will lift us up, encourage us, and raise our standards.

Ed Mylett says that the people you keep closest and spend the most time with should have something in their lives that you want. This makes sense. Who better to teach you how to acquire the skills, the qualities, the money, the characteristics, or the accolades than someone who already has them?

"It's better to hang out with people better than you. Pick out associates whose behavior is better than yours and you'll drift in that direction."
– WARREN BUFFETT

CHALLENGE

Write down the names of the five people you spend the most time with. Write down beside their names why they are in your life. Who of these people are you most comfortable discussing growth and ambition with? Are there any you can get together with to discuss taking your professional relationship to the next level? Your challenge is to contact any or all of those people and ask to start a mastermind group where you get together regularly to encourage and push each other to new levels in your lives.

ADVANCED CHALLENGE

Which of the five names was the most uncomfortable to write? I say "uncomfortable" because you knew as you wrote their name that they were the person you have been reading about for the last five minutes—the person who does not lift you up. For the next two weeks, you are going to give some increased space between you two and see how you feel about your level of ambition and desire for more out of life. I am confident that you will notice those attributes have been heightened and you will recognize that friend has been holding you back.

I don't mean to be callous about this situation; the merciful side of me would love to communicate my thoughts to this friend and give them another shot. Sadly, I tried it that way for almost forty years; not one of those friends was I able to change. Not once in all my years of mentoring, coaching, employing, and befriending have I witnessed that friend, when given one last chance, step up. Instead, I've seen more and more sadness, lost time, and feelings of discouragement and failure from the friend trying to pull that person up. If that friend wanted to come up, they would have already. Even more exciting, they will still have the chance as you level up and inspire them to even greater things—from afar.

Have strength in knowing that you are doing a great service to yourself and to that other person by putting some space between you. Allow both of you to become the people you are destined to be.

YOUR PARTNER

Let's talk about your spouse, your life partner, your long-term whatever—you know who I'm talking about! This is the most important choice of your life. **If you want real success in life, it can only be accessed if you have the right person at your side.**

The right person will lift you up, push you, inspire you, and fill you up in ways you must be filled if you want to go out and dominate the world. The wrong person will bring you down, tear you down, withhold the things you require, talk down to you, and make it near impossible to get ahead in life.

If you are already married to a downer, I highly recommend you increase communication and get some counseling. That person has great power in your life, and you need them to wield it for good. Do not go to them and demand changes; I think we both know how that conversation will go. Come to them in a loving manner and be vulnerable. Let them know the human you could be if they were to support and love you in a more positive manner. Commit to doing the same for them.

I could write a whole book for this section because it is vitally important. I recommend you read everything you can on improving your relationship and commit fully to making a change for the benefit of everyone in your family.

If you are not yet married, find that someone who will lift you up and be your running mate, not the ball and chain that destroys your chances of living the life you are working so hard for.

I don't go a day without recognizing how amazing Brooke is for me. She offers me so much love, patience, mercy, gentleness, care . . . and she truly makes me feel like the strongest, handsomest, most manly man on the planet. Because of the way she builds me up, I leave the house every day ready to conquer. A big part of why I do conquer is because I want to make her right! I want to show her proof that I am that man. It is my way of encouraging her to keep pushing me and loving me in that way.

Part of being that man is showing her the same love, respect, mercy, patience . . . that's what a real man does. Does this sound like a relationship you'd like for yourself? It is available to you, but it takes work. You need to commit to building your integrity and character, you need to not settle for someone for any of the wrong reasons (e.g., because they are hot, it is comfortable, you were lonely). **Finding the right mate is a prerequisite to real success.**

BEING VULNERABLE DOESN'T ALWAYS MEAN BEING EMOTIONAL

Just when you thought you were getting a handle on the vulnerability idea, I throw you this little curveball. While exploring your vulnerability, there will certainly be times of great emotion. Opening up to people through vulnerability will spark emotion and have you discovering hurts, scars, and pains you may not have known you were carrying. But with this beautiful process comes healing and deeper connections in your relationships. In these times, try not to hold back—embrace the healing in this journey.

I do believe there is a time and place for emotions, but business meetings are not one of them! (Please take note that I said "business meetings" and not just "business"). In business, there will be wonderful times of sharing your vulnerability that will once again create special connections, bonds, and trust—and things can get emotional. In business meetings however, I have found great success in always checking my emotions at the door.

In any negotiations or arguments, when I am faced with someone's emotions I am no longer confident we will be speaking in rational terms. Once emotions get involved, it has been my experience that rational thinking is gone. I learned the hard way that continuing a meeting as if it hadn't gotten emotional is the worst thing I could do; whatever rational arguments I might bring up can be used against me when filtered through emotional lenses. Because of emotion, I have seen brilliant, multi-million-dollar deals, clear win-wins for all parties, go up in flames. We have seen it in TV shows and movies, and I am here to say, it is incredibly accurate.

Many high-powered businesspeople have learned this. The negative side of bringing emotion to a meeting is what you will lose. It is rare that I take a second meeting with someone who brings heavy emotions to a business meeting (sometimes a second, but never a third). Time is our most scarce and precious resource. If I carved out time to have a meeting that abruptly ended when heavy emotions flared up, torpedoing the whole thing, why would I want to offer more of my most precious resource?

Of course, I do attempt to calm emotions and salvage the meeting. I listen until the person calms down. I try to remind them of the benefits of our dealings, and sometimes they come back around. But why put your fate fully in the hope of the person across the table being proficient at defusing bombs? Before every meeting, mentally prepare yourself to keep your emotions in check.

The scarier, deeper meaning to me in dealing with someone who is so emotional that it leaks into a critical business meeting is that they are likely one thousand times worse in their daily dealings. Is that someone I want using my name? Is that someone I want representing me or my business? How much will this negatively impact my life? How will that emotion negatively impact their future meetings and decisions?

I knew even early on that my choices were setting me up for success

...in any language.

CONCLUSION

Success is a choice. Every day you will be faced with an abundance of choices that lead to success or complacency. Recognize and accept that these choices are yours. What path you end on is up to you.

Seeing the world in this way is a massive first step in taking control of your destiny. The alternative is waiting, wishing, and hoping for success to fall into your lap. **You get to write your story by the choices you make.** Now put the time and effort into making the right choices and let's write your story as one of the greatest success stories of all time.

FAITH

"Faith is taking the first step even when you don't see the whole staircase."
— MARTIN LUTHER KING JR.

Faith can be one of the trickiest topics to write about in a book about success; yet you will find few books about success that do not broach the subject. I could not stay in integrity if I were to offer you all my principles of success without writing about faith.

To start, faith means far more than just a belief in a higher power. It required faith to buy this book. You had to have faith that I was someone who could help you on your journey. You had to have faith that the person who recommended this book wasn't out to lunch. And you must have faith to take my challenges and be consistent on your new path or you will not make any lasting change to your life.

Every step toward your massive goals requires consistent faith. Any goal that you cannot achieve within a few hours (which is virtually every goal) will require faith in the process, as you might only be moving inches forward each day. I can think of no better example of this than, once again, your workouts and diet.

For you to make real changes to your physique, you must daily follow your plan and have faith in the process. Your body will not change overnight. To measure how much each workout or each meal changed you physically is nearly impossible and certainly negligible. The trust that you are moving in the right direction, and that your efforts will payoff, is faith.

This is the main reason I believe faith and discipline are dependent on each other. **Faith without discipline is just empty words. Discipline without faith is a bullet train to nowhere.** To exercise and build strength in both results in an unstoppable force.

I am nothing without my faith.

DISCERNMENT

Have faith in your ability to discern right from wrong. You have had years of practice in learning from every situation you have ever put yourself in. You are more equipped than you likely give yourself credit for. It is time to lean into this wisdom with greater confidence.

Yes, you will still make mistakes. You are not perfect. But with practice and experience, your mistakes should no longer come with considerable downside (i.e., you should not be putting yourself in a "bet it all on red" situation).

A good chunk of my confidence comes from the trust I have in my ability to discern. When I make calculated decisions, I rely on my discernment to steer me on the right path, and I don't make a habit of looking back or questioning those decisions. I was once someone who did question myself often, and it led me in circles.

If we take the energy we spend on questioning ourselves and looking at the path we did not choose, and spend that energy on moving forward and committing to the path we are on, we will

experience levels of success and confidence that few experience in this lifetime.

"Living in the moment" has taken on new meaning for me since I started on my path to success. I once believed this philosophy had to do with wrangling in the daydreamer, but I learned it is all about our energy and where we focus it. How many of us, in any given moment, commit our full attention to what we are doing? Not only our attention, but how much of our focus, energy, strength, and ability?

Beyond the obvious distractions (thinking about what we will have for lunch, what's happening on social media right now, is my team playing tonight, how my base is looking on the current video game I kill time on, do I look funny in this shirt) we often don't even show up with our full attention because we brought in our daily baggage. Almost all of us have this constantly playing in the background: government concerns, health worries, family life, financial issues . . . all the anxieties we allow to take up space in our minds all day long.

If you can become someone who lives in the moment, who turns off all the background noise and learns to narrow your focus on the task right in front of you—well, you stand to inherit the earth.

"We should not fret for what is past, nor should we be anxious about the future; men of discernment deal only with the present moment."
– CHANAKYA

I also think of this principle as committing fully to my decisions. While playing golf last month, I recognized the value of this practice in all aspects of life. In golf, I would often decide on the shot I would take, but constantly wonder if it was the right move and not fully commit because I wasn't fully convinced . . . can you guess the outcome? It was never good.

I used this mindset technique to forever change my golf game. I now make a decision for the shot and commit to it fully. No second guessing, no wondering what would happen if I chose a different strategy, no thoughts about bunkers or hazards, and no negative thoughts about what I am about to do. The result was astounding! The ball often seems to go exactly where I want it to. I dropped 6–8 strokes off my game overnight! (If you aren't familiar with golf, that is an insane drop that takes most people, including myself, years to see.)

Why would you expect anything different in business, relationships, your health . . . if you only partially commit and are always watching the other avenues and questioning your choices, how do you expect to flourish? **If we give our full attention and commitment to anything, the results will always be far better than with a partial commitment.**

Notice that I didn't say it will guarantee success? There are far too many other factors at play to guarantee success with this principle, but that's not what is important here anyway. By using this practice in everything you do, you will always know that you gave it your all and you never need to wonder if it would have been a success if you had only committed yourself more.

What a beautiful lesson to share with our children! I remind my girls of this mindset technique all the time so they can find the sports and activities they will have a true passion for. If they only put 50 percent effort into a sport, how will they really know if they like it? Playing it with your full effort makes it a totally different game. I tell them that I don't mind them moving on from a sport as long as they can, with full integrity, tell me they gave it their all first.

DON'T MAKE DECISIONS BASED ON FEAR

"Where your focus goes, energy flows."
– TONY ROBBINS

Many of these principles, on their own, will change your life completely; this is one of those standalone principles, and one of the most critical principles in this book. Living in fear is the polar opposite to living for success. If you want to live a life marked by success, you must learn to catch yourself focusing on fear, creating responses based on fear, and using fearful language. Once you've been caught, you need to create routines and habits to call yourself on it, laugh it off, and start again with a positive focus.

Things to fear are real. I am not suggesting you are making them up or that pretending they aren't there will make them go away. I am telling you that if you want what I know you want out of this book and out of your life, you must learn to tell a different story about the scary stuff.

Planes do crash. That's a fact and it is horrifying. But if you focus too hard on planes crashing, you are going to shrink your world until you never consider boarding a plane. Continue focusing on how that plane could crash and kill you, even if you aren't on it, and I don't know how you get out of bed in the morning.

How about changing that story to say that the vast majority, really close to 100 percent of flights, don't crash, and that traveling by plane is the safest way to travel? Just like that, one fear off your list!

Like any new story we are going to tell ourselves, it isn't as easy as just saying it once. You will need to find the best way to get your new story in and your old story out. Repetition seems to work for the majority of humans and it has always worked for me. I catch myself anytime my thinking goes in a direction I don't like and I correct it. I find it helpful to laugh off the old way of thinking (you can always find a reason to frame that fearful thinking as silly). I make sticky notes to remind me of what my new story is everywhere I go. **It won't take as long as you think to fully change your story, just have faith and be persistent in replacing the old with the new.**

Focusing on the fear will always make the fear worse and more real. Whatever information you are looking for, you will find supportive evidence. If you are keeping a fear about why you shouldn't move forward with a business, you will find tons of supporting arguments. Your brain will not only remind you of all your failures in life, but it will also make sure you don't miss every story on social media, in movies, and all around you about how your plans will fail. The opposite way of thinking will produce the opposite results!

If you ask your brain to focus on all the reasons you will succeed, it will bring back all your memories of triumph. It will also highlight for you all the articles, stories, and posts about others who went for it and succeeded. **It is 100 percent your choice which way of thinking you want to focus on and which path you want your brain to take.**

This is our brains' reticular activating system (or RAS) at work. The RAS is a network of neurons at the base of our brainstem that filters information. Much like Siri (that helpful computer AI that answers the random questions we ask all day), our RAS delivers information in the way we ask for it. If we ask a question in a positive way, "Is air travel safe?" we will get positive answers that prove it's safety. If we ask in a fearful or negative way, "Do planes crash?" we will get back answers about how many planes have cashed, how many fatalities there were, and so on.

Your RAS does not filter results in a subjective way. It is critical to know how the RAS works so we don't create a path to misery through the way we ask questions.

This can be extremely empowering if you choose to use your RAS to your benefit. If you are mindful to always feed the RAS positively (always use positive diction, leading the RAS toward a positive answer), it can support you with non-stop positivity, examples, science, history, and proof that you will succeed in your endeavors.

Fun Story

Recently at Magnum, we received a bunch of new rules to follow from Health Canada. These rules and restrictions seemed frivolous. They didn't appear to help or protect the public at all, but just created more jobs for this government agency and cost Magnum hundreds of thousands of extra dollars per year.

As you can imagine, the meetings about these new regulations were not fun. Many times the meeting took a negative turn toward fear-based discussions and the feeling in the room was gross. We mostly spoke about things outside of our control and, big surprise, we felt powerless and scared. I constantly requested that we focus on action and what needed to be done, but these meetings were the most draining meetings we have had in years.

After three days of these meetings, I called a moratorium on any

Health Canada talks. I let everyone know that the discussions were far too fear-based; it had clearly taken a toll on everyone involved. When we scheduled our next meeting, days later, I set new rules about how the discussions would go.

"I want to hear solutions only from this point forward, and I want everyone to catch themselves if they are speaking through fear. **Let's focus on what we can control.**"

Because of these new rules, we laughed so much through these next meetings as we called each other out on fear talk and bringing up problems instead of solutions. We made such a fun game out of it that we left those next two meetings with huge smiles and concrete plans to act on. We fed our reticular activating systems with solutions and ways to move forward, and we were supported with the reasons the plans would work.

Things quickly changed. After those first meetings, I was wiped when I got home and didn't even want to come into work the next day. The final meetings were far more productive and fun and left us feeling energized and back in control. The facts were still the same, the only thing that changed was the story we made about them.

Fearful focus will destroy your opportunities to succeed. Focus instead on solutions and what is within your control. Catch yourself in fearful thought and stop yourself fast. The more time you commit to changing your thought patterns in this way, the more your brain will naturally focus on the positive and ensure the positive will become your reality.

"I love the man that can smile in trouble, that can gather strength from distress, and grow brave by reflection. Tis the business of little minds to shrink, but he whose heart is firm, and whose conscience approves his conduct, will pursue his principles unto death."
-THOMAS PAINE

IT'S NOT ME, IT'S YOU!

In the same way I perceived Health Canada breathing down my neck, we will find many situations where we feel targeted. When I am under attack, I never take it personally. When someone is "unloading" on me, whether that be leaving a rude comment for me on social media, flipping me the bird while driving (yeah, that's right, I'm bringing back '80s lingo), telling me off in person, or just being generally negative or rude toward me, I find it doesn't serve me even 1 percent to think it is personal; it never is!

I know who I am and I know the positivity I exude. I know that not everyone loves that positivity, and that my success and joy can make people sad about their station in life. While my circumstances might trigger them, it is 100 percent on them if they are going to act up. I don't need to spend a second thinking about how this might be my fault.

Remember, you can control you, but you can't control anyone else. You are responsible for your actions, not theirs.

The need to keep negativity from overtaking you is something I want to impart to my girls and all young people (though really it applies to all of us). I want to tell them that some of their friends will say it can't be done because they've never seen it done. If they keep slowing you down, you might need to replace them. Come to playabiggergame.com and find new friends! I joke, but I made this book and this business for the two of them and all the other high achievers out there who may not be living up to their potential because of the people they associate with. Don't limit your shine just because your friends prefer the dark.

Without question, the number one place this will help most of you is on social media. Isn't it so sad that we will instantly look past hundreds of likes and wonderful comments so we can stew on the one negative comment that came from someone who doesn't even know us? This tells us plainly that our brains were not prepared for social media, and the best thing to do is stay away from it. But if you are going to press on, remember this tool and use it as often as needed: **Block and Walk!** Block the person and walk away. Don't forget to forget them too!

That negativity being thrown your way has nothing to do with you, but the longer you bathe in it, the more it will infect you. On social media, it is very easy to block the person and forget they ever existed. In person, I love having a few defusing phrases on hand in the event I am targeted. You might like to try using the classic, "Are you okay?" or "Those are great shoes!" or my favorite, "I hope you feel very blessed today!" Replying with a curveball and positivity usually throws someone off balance and deescalates the situation.

Of course, there are many times when the person is simply on fire inside and the safest approach is to say nothing and simply walk away. There is no defeat in that and, while you might think your ego takes a hit from walking away from a fight, I have found it does the opposite. I revel in my strength for walking away from an unwinnable situation. Why would you, a person of intelligence, class, and success, stoop down to get in a junkyard fight with someone who likely has nothing to lose? And besides, this had nothing to do with you, you were just unfortunate enough to be standing there as the tornado passed through.

For your ego, just remember that the only people who would side with a maniac are other maniacs. Anyone with intelligence who is watching will admire your strength and wisdom. Do you think Mark Cuban is going to waste his time replying to rudeness from a stranger? Then why would you?

REFRAMING HOW WE CARRY STRESS

"Rule number one is, don't sweat the small stuff. Rule number two is, it's all small stuff."
– ROBERT ELIOT

I will not be the first person to suggest stress is like carrying baggage. Allowing stress and worry to rule your life is like waking up fresh and ready in the morning and choosing to grab a forty-pound backpack that you will carry with you all day (yes, I know some backpacks are full of useful tools for living, but these are filled with rocks). Is it any surprise that we are exhausted by noon? Is it any surprise that it isn't easy to focus? That's a lot of baggage we are carrying. We must discover ways to leave the baggage where it is so we can walk unencumbered into our day.

Many tips in this book will help you reframe to let this baggage go, but I want to share what has been my most powerful strategy:

finding God. I always found it so interesting that the top self-help minds have always suggested that we "find God." When I heard Brian Tracy and Tony Robbins speak of it in person, it led me to searching for exactly how God can help with business, mindset, and stress relief. Because of what I discovered, **when I am asked the number one piece of advice to young entrepreneurs who want to go big, I always say "find God."** If you are a non-believer, please stay with me—this is not a "Christian rant."

If you want to do big things in life (which I know you do or you wouldn't be reading this book), I mean truly remarkable works, you are hindering your chances of success beyond measure by believing the world is 100 percent on your shoulders.

This line of thinking is too much for the average person to bear, but you want to be far above average. The stress of knowing that your mortgage payment and family food is 100 percent dependent on you, your strength, your abilities, and your work ethic is a burden that cripples most people.

At the time of me writing these words, I have over a hundred family mortgages and over four hundred mouths to feed that are counting on me to keep successful businesses going. That's pretty simple math to take whatever stress the average person feels, multiply it by somewhere between one hundred and four hundred, and lay it on my shoulders.

No, I am not a superhero, and as far as I know I am not a sociopath who wouldn't notice the difference. The reason Tracy and Robbins and all the greats tell you to find God is to know that there is a bigger power at play, bigger plans at work, and someone far bigger and more powerful to carry the baggage. And the best part is, God wants to carry it!

"Do not be anxious about anything, but in every situation, by prayer and petition, with thanksgiving, present your requests to God. And the peace of God, which transcends all understanding, will guard your hearts and your minds in Christ Jesus."

PHILIPPIANS 4:6-7

What I am offering here is far more than just advice or a motto or a tactic to employ. God is offering to take on all your stress, anxiety, and burdens, but He offers far more to anyone who searches for Him.

I won't harp on this point any further, but I will leave you with one question: **IF there was a God and He was willing to take all this off your shoulders, how much further could you go in life carrying none of these burdens, stresses, and worries?**

Take the time to imagine and visualize what your life would be like with none of that on your shoulders. How would your energy be all day? At what point in the day do you think you would slow down, or do you think you could sprint from morning until night? How would that lack of stress and baggage impact your relationships (think about your spouse or future spouse, your clients, your friends, your investors . . .)?

You and I both know there is also a compounding effect to this energy, focus, strength, endurance, and success. Where would you be in five years without the load on your shoulders? Ten years? Twenty years? So isn't it worth taking ten to twenty hours to look into this opportunity and decide if God is someone you'd like to work with?

CHALLENGE

Make a list. If there was a God who asked you to hand over all your burdens, stresses, and worries, what would be on your list? Now take time to imagine those things no longer exist—they no longer weigh you down or burden you. How much better would you sleep at night with none of this baggage? Imagine yourself waking up each morning and not putting that load on. How is your energy? What are you like to be around? Do you think others will notice a difference in you?

ADVANCED CHALLENGE

Find someone in your life that you admire or respect who has God in their life. Ask them out to coffee or lunch and find out what God means to them and what role God plays in their life. Keep an open mind and form your own opinion from your own research. (Sadly, as I have had many of these discussions, most people's opinions were created from social media or handed down from a parent. Let's not assume their views are right for you—or right at all. Form your own opinion.) Remember the most important points of choosing the person you are going to speak with: you admire and respect them. Ideally, you also notice that they don't carry baggage like others—you will be more eager to learn their secrets.

"For I know the plans I have for you, declares the Lord, plans to prosper you and not to harm you, plans to give you hope and a future."
JEREMIAH 29:11

PRO TIP FOR REDUCING STRESS

I learned this one in my early twenties and it made a massive difference to my stress levels! When looking for a parking spot at a busy place (the mall, church, Walmart), I used to stress so hard trying to get a "dream" spot. I swear that I learned this terrible habit as a boy and heard the story in my head, "Real men get the best spots."

Well, I changed that story. I look for the spot furthest away! Here's what is so great about this practice: no one is trying to get those spots, so they are usually empty. It takes me no time or stress to find a spot. But the best part is, I then get extra exercise by walking.

New goal: by the time you finish reading this book, you have discovered multiple ways to leave this baggage behind as you sprint toward success.

PARALYSIS BY ANALYSIS

"In a moment of decision, the best thing you can do is the right thing to do, the next best thing is the wrong thing, and the worst thing you can do is nothing."

– THEODORE ROOSEVELT

I learned the term *paralysis by analysis* in university and it was burned into my memory as the worst outcome. That said, we have all done it! We spend countless hours analyzing the data, researching the history, making options and forecasting the results, only to go back and revisit the data, quadruple check the options, reimagine the outcomes . . . and do absolutely nothing. It is easier and more comfortable to spend time in the thinking room than in the unknown where execution takes place. **Without the doing, all the planning and thinking have zero value. If you take nothing else from this section, I want you to remember to take action.**

Of course, planning, visualizing, hypothesizing, analyzing, and researching have a critical role in any venture. There is not a definitive amount of time that is too little or too much spent analyzing the choices—every venture and every decision has its own variables and timelines. I have personally seen, and experienced firsthand, how a lack of time put into thinking things through and visualizing outcomes can kill a venture. So take the appropriate amount of time to think about the outcome. But now we come to the reason paralysis by analysis falls within the Faith principle.

"The most difficult thing is the decision to act, the rest is merely tenacity."
– AMELIA EARHART

To know when the timing is right to pull the trigger on your plans, you must have faith in yourself. You must have faith that you have put in the sufficient amount of time planning and preparing. If you still believe this is the right move and will lead to success, you must have the faith that you have used your wisdom, discernment, and skills to reach the conclusion that will succeed.

Any extra time analyzing past this point will likely have you questioning everything, and since you have already reached the limit of what your wisdom, discernment, and skills can tell you, you are now outside your realm of understanding and the fog will set in. How likely are you to hit the target through the fog?

This is a critical moment to be mindful of the story you are telling yourself. If your story is about likely failure, your brain will find endless data to prove that. If you change your story and speak of how this will be a success, your brain will now find the data to back that up. Which story do you want to tell?

> "Thinking too much leads to paralysis by analysis. It's important to think things through, but many use thinking as a means of avoiding action."
> – ROBERT HERJAVEK

SOMEONE HAS TO WIN, WHY NOT YOU?

If you are looking for a technique to get you moving forward and taking action on your plans, here it is. This is another of my favorite mindset-shifting, reframing principles, and a most profound question to ask yourself: Someone has to win, why not me?

Someone has to be the leader. Someone has to make a great business. Someone has to date that very attractive human over there. Why not me?

Just asking the question gets you halfway there. ANY answer you give to these questions that isn't positive is simply an excuse. I hate excuses and I call myself on it every time I try to pass one off. The only real answer to these questions is "there is no reason it can't be me."

When applied properly, this question should get you out of bed every day. It should help you stand back up when you have fallen. It should be the question to revert to constantly to bring yourself back to the critical mindset that you CAN do whatever it is you need to do. I'd say this is worth at least six sticky notes.

In the next chapter we are going to redefine what success means to you, but right now I need to mention that asking this mindset question, stepping up to the plate over and over, will not guarantee success as you now know it. But it guarantees that you have a shot at success.

> "You miss 100 percent of shots you don't take."
> – WAYNE GRETZKY
> – MICHAEL SCOTT

Let me rephrase this spectacular quote: **if you never step up to the plate, you have a 0 percent chance at success.** Almost every person who I meet who doesn't step up to the plate has a fear-based scarcity mindset. They believe they will likely fail, so why try? "I only have one chance," they say. This isn't true (they will never take that one chance anyway).

The truth is, the world is made up primarily of people with that mindset (I'd honestly and conservatively say 99.999 percent of people think this way) and the people willing to step up to the plate can have as many swings as they'd like, since almost no one else wants their shot! I want you to ask this question: Why not me? Step up to the plate and take a swing. Maybe it isn't a homerun, but on the tenth swing you make a little contact. With every at bat, you will learn. You will adapt, implement new strategies, focus differently . . . this is how you will succeed.

My friend and mentor Rory Vaden is never afraid to discuss his faith. I love how Rory describes his faith in himself and his work ethic and how he will never fear taking a chance:

> The other place that my faith comes from is my work ethic.
>
> Success ultimately is a numbers game.
>
> I have been in enough situations and environments to know that if I can outwork everybody, I will probably have results that are greater than most people in any environment and any industry.
>
> I could go be a real estate agent, a mortgage broker, a car salesperson, an insurance professional, or even I could start my own medical center.
>
> No matter what industry, if I trust myself to work and have a strong work ethic, I have faith that I can be successful.[*]

Next, I will discuss how to be done with the concept of failure. The way I see it, and the way I live, I never fail.

---

[*] Vaden, Rory. "Have faith in these 3 areas to achieve success in sales." Rory-Vaden.com/blog/sales/have-faith-in-these-3-areas-to-achieve-success-in-sales/.

I DO NOT FAIL. I SUCCEED OR I LEARN

"Develop success from failures. Discouragement and failure are two of the surest stepping stones to success."
– DALE CARNEGIE

I don't know if this is a very advanced mindset or if I was just really slow to learn it, but this one took me a good forty years to truly understand. This is an incredibly powerful mindset that fully eliminates hesitancy to give things a try. It also eliminates all the regret and negative self-talk if things don't go exactly as I had planned or hoped.

Before I start explaining the method, let's be clear on something—eliminating hesitancy doesn't mean I jump headfirst into any and every opportunity before looking where I am going. I have accumulated wisdom and knowledge for good reason, and I use it always. But many people suffer from paralysis by analysis and never seem to take a step toward their goals. Once I have done my research, thought of possible outcomes, and weighed the risk, I am happy to jump, commit fully, and see where I land.

If you truly don't believe you are the right person to be making the moves you are thinking of making, you are correct. This mindset method is predicated on you already taking some time to analyze your options and deciding if you are the right person to be trying what you are about to try. **You do not have to be 100 percent certain about this, but you can't be 0 percent!**

Risk/reward is also critically important to weigh out with all big decisions. If you are putting big money on the line, for example, and the payoff if you succeed is relatively small, and the likelihood of things going your way is minute, that sounds like a bad move.

Calculating the downside to your venture (i.e., if things don't play out how you hope they will) is always an important step before making your decision. Ideally, the worst-case scenario won't cost you a fortune. Some big payoffs will require big risk—this is a massive topic and might be something I tackle in a future book. But for now, I will give you credit to say you know how to calculate the amount of risk you find acceptable.

If you have determined you could be the right person for this move and your risk/reward is acceptable, having an "I can't lose" mindset is glorious.

Fun Story

I once started a company called Performance Panties. As you might have gathered from the name, it was performance underwear. It might surprise you to hear that it was for both women and men!

We created amazing underwear made of breathable, stretchy, soft, comfortable fabrics—almost everyone who put them on said it was the best pair of underwear they owned.

Magnum had been around for a good ten years and was already extremely successful—we had truly built a brand. My marketing and graphics teams were at the top of their game and were excited for this new challenge. I had hundreds of beautiful, healthy, kind, popular athletes on my team who were willing and excited to take part in any project I was going to start. These athletes were real influencers. They were known and idolized in their communities.

So we had the right product, we had amazing marketing, we had an army of incredible influencers, our pricing was in line with the market . . . yet the business was a flop. What happened? I am confident there is more than one reason and I certainly learned many lessons through this process, but I will argue the main answer is in the first sentence of my story. I gave men too much credit; I thought we lived in the time in history when it would showcase the confidence in our manhood to wear underwear called "panties." I was wrong.

Even with everything else looking like it would make this business skyrocket to success, missing just a couple of fundamentals cost the business everything.

I did not fail. That might be hard for many reading this to see, because the company is not around anymore and it did not make money; but *failure* is not a factual term, it is a mindset. Failing and not succeeding are two very different things (although I find it hilarious that when I typed in *not succeeding*, Microsoft Word underlined it for grammar and suggested I change it to *failing*!).

I learned an incredible lesson that did not cost me a fortune and I am confident saved me from losing much more in future endeavors. Maybe even more importantly, it didn't hurt my confidence or slow me down from looking at my next project and the project after that.

Getting an education is not cheap. One way or another, it will cost you something to learn. I learned a ton from this unsuccessful business, and it didn't break my bank or my back.

"Every problem is a gift—without problems we would not grow."
– TONY ROBBINS

CONFIDENCE

A great deal of my confidence stems from my faith. I figured it was best to keep this until the end of the faith section because the more you master the topics in this section, the greater your confidence will become. Let's highlight all the ways your confidence should grow through faith.

First, believing there is a higher power in this world who has plans that are far greater than yours, and whose power is billions of times greater, **you can be confident that the weight of the world does not need to sit on your shoulders.**

Next, you can be confident in your discernment. Your path through life has been 100 percent unique and has led you to know and understand many things. You can be confident in your unique wisdom that guides you, gives you gut feelings, ignites your passions, draws you to certain people and away from others . . . **You were made to be on the path you are on right now and you can be confident you will know what direction to go from here.**

You can be confident you will have less stress from now on. Your circumstances may not have changed, but you are now better equipped to look at stress differently and manage it better. You can be confident that with less stress dragging you down every moment of every day you will have more energy to focus on the things that matter, and you can expect to get ahead in life faster (assuming you direct that energy toward the right stuff).

You can be confident in the decisions you are going to make. Once you have done the research and made plans, you can move forward in action and not be held back by over-analyzing. You can be confident that someone will be the winner! Someone will have the successful business, someone will win the prize, and someone will end up on top. If you have put in the work, done the analysis, prepared, and made the right moves, you can be confident that someone will be you.

And finally, you can also be confident that even if things don't work out perfectly, you will learn from the situation and move forward wiser than before, having increased your likelihood of success on your next move.

Fun Story: Being Rejected Changed My Life!

I was thirteen years old when I asked out the school's sweetheart, Laura Thomas. As you recall from earlier in the book, at thirteen I had absolutely no business asking this girl out! This moment in my life was truly heartbreaking, but one of the most valuable pivoting points in my life and one of my greatest confidence boosters. Let me tell you how I took this rejection and created a better story.

First off, my story isn't about Laura. She was very sweet and I am sure there was good reason every boy in the school wanted to date her, but for me, she was a symbol. She symbolized the Kelly Kapowski of my school (for my *Saved by the Bell* fans). Only a real man, only the best of the best should step up to the plate. I love that I took that chance. I love that even at that age, I was applying the principle that "someone has to win, why not me?" This was not my time, but it certainly put me on a new path.

I was devastated that she said no. For years I tried to figure out if I could have said or done anything different. Of course, the answer is no. It was not the circumstances; it was who I was. A few years later, when I started changing my story, I vowed to become the man who would always have the confidence to step up to that plate, but also be the man who always gets the yes.

If you have a hurt in your life, something that has always pained you—likely the very thing that came to your mind as you started reading this sentence—that is the perfect hurt to use to create your new story. I now use that horrible feeling of rejection to work harder, in every aspect of my life, to make sure that rejection never happens again.

Of course I am not limiting this to asking girls out! That part of my story ended over twenty years ago when I asked out the most amazing woman on the planet (spoiler alert: she said yes). It would be the same feeling of rejection if the bank said no, the client said no, or anyone else I wanted a yes from said no. I use this every day to workout harder, to eat clean, to read more, to learn more, and to work smarter and harder, and I have faith that these actions are making me the man I always wanted to be. Because of this, I have the confidence I need to succeed. **I will get the yes I desire because I will do everything it takes to make that yes come easily.**

"To one who has faith, no explanation is necessary. To one without faith, no explanation is possible."
– THOMAS AQUINAS

PRINCIPLE 4

SERVICE

"There are three ways to ultimate success: The first way is to be
kind. The second way is to be kind. The third way is to be kind."
– MISTER ROGERS

I believe my main purpose in life is to serve. I serve God, and I
serve my fellow man. I believe that every blessing and talent bestowed
on me was for the sole purpose of serving and making this world
a better place for others. I believe the more I serve and give to the
people of this world, the more I am blessed and the more this world
wants to see me receive more. I believe I am in a beautiful cycle of
giving and receiving, and I never want that cycle to end!

I once believed serving others was solely to help them and that
I would receive nothing in return. That couldn't be further from
the truth. The truth is, I receive so much warmth, joy, excitement,
purpose, wisdom, hugs, and so much more every time I give. I feel
like I give for selfish purposes now!

Serving others is one of the rare times these days that we aren't
self-focused. We live in a time when we are constantly thinking of
how we look, how everything makes us feel, how others feel about
us, what we should eat next, what we should post about today, and

on and on. Serving others allows us to put aside our self-thoughts and focus on someone else.

Studies show that serving others has major physical and mental health benefits. **Reducing depression, lowering blood pressure, boosting self-esteem, and living longer are just a few proven benefits of serving others.** There is also a natural sense of belonging, new friendships, strengthened relationships, increased positivity . . . There are more benefits than I have space to write.

I do not serve for show. When I first started serving others, I would often make sure it was seen. There was an emptiness, a gross feeling I would have as I realized I was serving for praise (whether that be on social media or when it would "naturally" come up in conversation). I believe the greatest rewards are reserved for those who serve in silence.

When I serve, when I give, when I support in silence, I am filled with something beautiful. I feel as though I am feeding my character and soul. Not only do others receive the benefits of my service, but I too receive so much. Once again, I receive the incredible feelings you get when you know you are doing what you have been sent here to do—the fulfillment of your true purpose for being. There are few feelings in our lives that can match this. This is a feeling worth chasing, always.

"So when you give to the needy, do not announce it with trumpets, as the hypocrites do . . . to be honored by others. Truly I tell you, they have received their reward in full."
– JESUS CHRIST, MATTHEW 6:2

One of my favorite action actors of all time is Dwayne "The Rock" Johnson. The Rock is quickly becoming one of the most charitable, giving actors of all time. When asked why he is so committed to giving and serving his fellow man, he replied, **"Service to others is the rent we pay for the room we have here on earth."** I can't help but love that one of his top-selling Under Armour shirts reads RENT'S DUE.

BE UNAPOLOGETICALLY YOU

"You have a vital role to play in the unfolding destiny of the world. You are, therefore, morally obliged to take care of yourself."
– JORDAN PETERSON

You have been put on this planet to serve in your own unique way. You, being uniquely you, are a gift to this world. Sadly, we live in the age of social media, and whether we admit it or not, we are all being algorithmed and conditioned to look the same, like the same things, and fall in line in every way.

Once again, I will encourage you to distance yourself from social media and break the hold it has on you and the path it is pushing you toward. You were made in a perfectly specific way, and that is the exact person this world needs.

But while you were created with the perfect recipe, you have not finished baking yet! The person you were meant to be is not the person you are today. It is up to you to constantly learn, grow, and expand your mind. **The world is in desperate need of you fulfilling your potential.**

Your shape, characteristics, history, strength, skin, core, and health are all unique. Why would any of us ever assume that these unique qualities are anything but perfect? I am here to tell you that this world needs you, exactly who you were made to be, not a "version" of you constructed out of things you've seen on the internet.

If you add this core belief to your arsenal, think of the confidence it can offer you in every situation you will face. To know, with certainty, that every experience you have had that has made you into the person you are today had its purpose. To know, with certainty, that you are today who you are supposed to be and where you are supposed to be. This is the spot where you can be confident you were supposed to start and build from. Now we are going to make you the best version of you. **You are the human that no one has ever been before!**

STANDARDS VS. EXPECTATIONS

I am about to save you a ton of pain that most people will experience as they set incredible new standards for their lives and try to impose those standards on others—just don't! I sadly must report that it took me 5–10 years, and many broken relationships, to learn this lesson. A great way to live as a high achiever is to **set high standards for yourself but hold others to low expectations.**

Setting high standards for yourself is an absolutely beautiful thing, but don't forget all that has happened in your life to bring you to the place where you are setting these standards. Your trials, tribulations, experiences, education, determination, discipline, ambition, triumphs . . .

your unique story has brought you to the place where you want way more out of life and are prepared to do what it takes to achieve more.

Of course I want you to surround yourself with other high achievers, and naturally you want to bring your friends and family on that part of the journey. Some of them will see the example you are setting and will love watching you shine so much that they jump on board for the ride. And since I love communication, I welcome you to discuss your life changes and standards with others you care about and invite them on the journey with you.

But I recommend you do this in the most loving and gentle way you know how. If they don't sign up for the ride at that point, any efforts you put into dragging them along will not only negatively impact your relationship in a huge way but will also take much of the energy you should be using to move yourself forward in life.

I recognize that "low expectations" has very bad connotations, and I accept that. Having low expectations of the people around me allows me to love them for who they are and be pleasantly surprised when they overachieve.

The idea of having high expectations for the people in my life sounds really good on paper, but in reality, I have only seen it end in disappointment, failure, and sadness. Remember, I am talking about your close friends and family. As you set new standards for yourself and start living by the principles in this book, you are going to invite new people into your life who are going to propel you forward in your new chapter. These are the people you can push and expect to be pushed in return. These are the high achievers you can hold to higher standards and expect more from. These are the people who have willingly signed up for this go-getter lifestyle and who will welcome the accountability.

In summary, reach for the moon in the new standards you set for yourself. Don't place those high expectations on the people who are currently in your life (if you want them to stay in your life). Find others with a similar mindset, then focus and drive and push each other to reach even higher levels than you had imagined. Now go become that amazing person I know you can be.

> "I'm not in this world to live up to your expectations and you're not in this world to live up to mine."
> – BRUCE LEE

If you don't have a place to find other high achievers to go through life with, come share in my community. Playabiggergame.com was created to bring these world leaders together and facilitate growth, wisdom-sharing, accountability, inspiration, motivation, and in every way to help us all play a bigger game.

LEARN TO LISTEN

For most of my life I was a terrible listener. I suppose, through my arrogance, I thought my opinions were so valuable that I needed to speak way more than I needed to listen. Do you know people like that? How quickly did you create an unfavorable opinion of that person the more they rambled on or injected their thoughts into every discussion?

Today, I try to never offer my thoughts until I am asked (I am still far from perfect at this, but I am seeing progress and I am loving the journey). **If no one is asking for your thoughts and opinions, what makes you think they will listen if you start sharing them anyway?** That was a life-changing question for me and I encourage you to read it again. If they aren't asking, their mind is likely closed off to any answer you could give. If they ask for your opinion or advice, they will be listening and are far more likely to absorb and use what you say.

The more I practiced entering conversations with this plan, the more I listened and absorbed all that was spoken. I love learning, and listening is an obvious opportunity to learn. I actively listened, I asked deeper questions, and I developed stronger relationships. Instead of just hearing one sentence about an experience, I asked how it made them feel, why it made them feel that way, whether they chose to do it again . . . this is insightful stuff into the human mind and the human condition.

Often in these conversations people open up. Together, we discover how their past played a critical role in how they act today—often in an adverse way. Not only do we help someone make a positive change, but you can imagine how it bonds us.

The more you know the inner thoughts and workings of the people around you, the better your chances and opportunities are to influence them. By spending time listening, you are showing your level of care. When people feel cared for, they are more likely to open up even more and to accept the guidance of the person who cares.

Imagine how much this principle alone can impact your career. How much easier is it to get promoted, improve corporate culture, sell something, and be heard if you are making these real connections with your superiors, your coworkers, and your clients.

Fun Fact

My wife is an excellent listener. For years I've witnessed her using this technique and the results are always astounding to me. The quieter she is, the more people assume she has brilliant things to say, even if they never ask her to speak! It takes wisdom and confidence to just listen.

Now Brooke is brilliant, so when she does speak, it just encourages the gossip about her intelligence and mystique! It takes her very few words to make a massive impact.

CHALLENGE

Enter into a conversation today and plan to not offer any opinions or thoughts unless asked. You will need to get a strong mindset before you enter the conversation so you will be prepared to hold your tongue! My dream for you is that you have at least one conversation where you are almost completely silent. This will build resiliency and strength that you didn't know you had. You will also find peace in this, as you now focus on listening and truly taking in what the speaker is saying.

You can learn something from everyone. If you remember this and truly believe it, imagine how much more intensely and intentionally you will be listening.

ADVANCED CHALLENGE

Be prepared to ask multiple follow-up questions and uncover deep meaning in any given story. If someone tells you they went to an Alanis Morissette concert last night and had a great time, ask why they chose that concert. Did they listen to Alanis growing up? Did hearing her music spark old memories? (This is a great spot to ask deeper questions about the memories.) How did it feel to experience those memories again? Do you think others in the crowd were having the same experience? How did that manifest?

Another Fun Fact

I took Brooke to an Alanis Morissette concert last month. I would not say either of us are big fans and neither of us ever go to concerts (this might have been my third concert ever). I remember Alanis's music fondly because the '90s were awesome and I love nostalgia, so we went and sat front row, center stage.

We were surrounded by hardcore fans and we loved seeing how her music sparked joy and wild emotions in so many people. Brooke and I will forever carry the hilarious memory of the lady standing next to me, who had a fair amount to drink (no judgment, but it makes the story funnier), screaming at the top of her lungs at Alanis, who was only around nine feet from us and starting in on a slow, quiet ballad: "I love you, Alanis! You got me through so much. So much, Alanis. You got me through so much!!! Alanis . . . so much!!!" You think Brooke and I will ever forget that amazing night?

WHAT ARE YOU WILLING TO SACRIFICE?

Success comes at a high price. I regularly sit down to list out what I am willing to sacrifice for success, and what I am not. I filter this question through the mindset that my life is dedicated to service. That filter is so important to me, because it makes the answer come more easily.

> "Great achievement is usually born of great sacrifice, and is never
> the result of selfishness."
> – NAPOLEON HILL

My sacrifices themselves are now a form of service to humanity. The more time I spend improving myself, reading, getting educated, enhancing my health . . . the better I will be at positively impacting this world. Can you see how backing up my plans with this conviction sets me up for unwavering focus and determination?

Spending time answering this question will also help you quickly navigate through the many times in your life you will be pulled in multiple directions. In knowing both my goals and what I was willing to give up to reach them, I easily said no to hundreds of invitations to the bars and nightclubs in my younger years.

So many invitations require a choice between the path we are on and a path going the opposite direction. Many of the invitations I declined would have derailed my workouts, my eating habits, or my time focused on education and reading, or put me in situations where my integrity might get called into question.

Creating this list will also help you see the things in your life that are most important to you. It might go without saying, but my wife and my two girls are second only to God on my list. Nothing gets priority over those four, and it makes decisions easy when they are involved.

Finally, I want to let you in on my own personal mindset when it comes to sacrifice. I suspect this line of thinking won't resonate with everyone, but it can be an incredibly powerful tool. Every time I make a sacrifice toward my goals and future, I take a moment to truly celebrate. I also love considering how many people in the world would be willing to make these sacrifices, because I know there aren't many.

If you aren't willing to do more than what most people are willing to do, how can you expect results greater than what most people experience?

It might sound like I am comparing myself to others, but I am simply reminding myself to do what others are not willing to do. Go longer and further than the majority. If I do that, I can expect more from my life.

One of my favorite billionaires is Mark Cuban. Because of his work on *Shark Tank*, always looking to educate and inspire entrepreneurs, I grew so much respect for him. Mark is never afraid to give it to you straight. Here are some candid thoughts on sacrifice from Mark Cuban:

> It is called working you're a** off. The difference is what you are willing to sacrifice. For every writer who wants balance in their life, there is a guy like me who gives up a lot to make their dreams come true. There is always going to be someone out there that knows they have to compensate for maybe having less talent with harder work and preparation.

CHALLENGE

Create your list of the top five to ten things you know you will need to sacrifice at times to keep you on your new path. These are usually time absorbers. The list usually includes bars, clubs, dinners out, TV time, and drinking time. Remember, I am not asking you to fully remove these things from your life, only to take note of them and get yourself mentally prepared to drop them more often than you are used to.

Now list the 5–10 things that are most important to your life that you are not willing to sacrifice. These are your top priorities and will trump anything that comes up.

ADVANCED CHALLENGE

In the next three days, find at least one opportunity to say no to something on your sacrifice list. Make it something challenging— not one of the items you always say no to anyway, but something you would like to say yes to.

Choose to invest that time in you instead.

Knowing that you have said no to something you wanted to do should give you drive to use that time wisely. It should energize you to know that you made this positive sacrifice. Take an extra minute to bathe in that victory. Recognize that missing whatever it was you said no to was not the end of the world. Recognize that the FOMO didn't end you. Take in the endorphins and serotonin that come with making a positive choice and an investment into your future. This win will make the next wins even easier.

Most importantly, **you must now use that time wisely.** You sacrificed something good. Don't squander that newly earned time on TV or social media. Use it for reading, developing, creating, exercising . . . Remind your brain that instead of wasting time, you did something amazing!

"There's a choice that we have to make as people, as individuals. If you want to be great at something, there's a choice you have to make. We all can be masters at our craft, but you have to make a choice. What I mean by that is, there are inherent sacrifices that come along with that. Family time, hanging out with friends, being a great friend, being a great son, nephew, whatever the case may be. There are sacrifices that come along with making that decision."
– KOBE BRYANT

CONFIDENCE

Confidence is ultimately a byproduct of knowing who you are. I suppose I could have written *real* confidence is a by-product of knowing who you are, as there are many young people, my younger self included, who experience false confidence. My purpose in giving you this book is to help you build up real confidence, so I will refrain from discussion on the artificial stuff!

Serving others will enhance your confidence. As I mentioned at the beginning of this chapter, serving others will feed your soul and give you those special feelings you can only get when you are in alignment with your true purpose for living. The more you live in that space, the greater your confidence will build every moment. Just think of what I am saying—you are spending time doing what you are on this planet to do, which very few people experience for even a moment in their lives—how would your confidence not increase?

Be intentional about discovering who you really are, because that is the person this world needs. The closer you find yourself to becoming that person, the greater your confidence will increase. This is a beautiful cycle of service, self-awareness, and confidence growth; once you start tumbling, lean into it and enjoy the ride!

DON'T SHOVE YOUR AWESOME LIFESTYLE DOWN EVERYONE'S THROAT

A word of warning: **You are about to see real improvements in your life.** I want you to share this with your friends and family, of course. But this section is so important because I have seen many people who start to taste success alienate themselves by sharing it in a negative way.

Take fitness as an example. I believe we all know someone who started on a new fitness journey and immediately started to experience and feel the benefits of their healthier lifestyle (this part I love!). But how did they share it with their friends and family? Did they let others notice and inquire about why they are glowing or looking so good? Or did they start judging you for eating this or that and asking you why you don't workout, "because you really should"?

This world has been conditioned to believe real change happens overnight, and in an effort to prove we have experienced this life-altering change, we want to aggressively show it off tomorrow. Almost inevitably, this ends in loneliness and failure.

I encourage you to let your success speak for itself—you don't need to give it a voice. It will take time, and if people aren't noticing, take that as a challenge to work harder so they can't help but notice! If it is in your career, working harder, putting in more time, dressing for success—these things are going to be very hard not to notice. If it is health, hitting the gym, making healthy food choices, going for extra walks—not only will they notice how you are committing your time, but if you stick with it long enough, they will have to notice the transformation of your energy and physique.

We want to keep the people who are close to us as cheerleaders, not rivals. Taking a position of encouragement and gentleness, and letting our success speak for itself, will always draw people closer. Remember that the things in their life holding them back from the successes you are experiencing are their issues, and if they aren't willing to put those issues aside long enough to ask for input and assistance, why on earth do we think they will accept it if we shove it down their throats?

If you need to brag to someone, you reach out to me and tell me how you are changing your life. It would be an honor to be your cheerleader! Tag us on social media with #playabiggergame and let me and the community encourage you!

I love the headline on this Japanese article—
not that I can read what the rest of it says.

CONCLUSION

Taking on the attitude that serving others is our true purpose on this planet will serve you in your quest for real success. Serving others will expedite the process of understanding who you really are and what truly lights you up.

There may be no greater service to this world than the sacrifices you will make on your journey to high achievement. Know that sacrifice is necessary and recognize the things in life you are and are not willing to sacrifice.

As you lean into the service that excites you, you will find yourself in greater alignment with your integrity, and your confidence will increase. As you become this aligned, improved version of yourself, people are going to be drawn to you and your power and your influence will soar. Recognizing this rise in your power and influence will become a great accountability force in your life. Using this to keep you on your path of integrity will serve you well.

Now go, share some positivity and love and serve this world by becoming the unstoppable human you were sent here to be.

"You, my brothers and sisters, were called to be free. But do not use your freedom to indulge the flesh; rather, serve one another humbly in love. For the entire law is fulfilled in keeping this one command: 'Love your neighbor as yourself.'"
– GALATIANS 5:13–14

GRATITUDE

"Gratitude is not only the greatest of virtues but the parent of all others."
– MARCUS TULLIUS CICERO

Def.
The quality of being thankful; readiness to show
appreciation for and to return kindness.

Gratitude is a virtue that will change your whole world. In our consumer society, it is so easy for us to get caught up in what we wish we had and be jealous of those who have what we want. The more time I spend being grateful for what I already have, the less I can even describe the extreme abundance in my life.

I promise you that the more time you spend on this principle of gratitude, the more wonderful your world will be, and you will radiate beauty in a way very few do. You will become a magnet for love, appreciation, respect, generosity, and success.

We live in a world where most of us don't appreciate something until it is taken away from us. When is the last time we were grateful for our freedom, the air we breathe, the fact that we woke up this morning? If I told you that these were going to be taken away from you tomorrow, how would you change the way you lived today? How many other gifts and blessings are in your life that you don't show gratitude for?

I have news for you, they WILL be taken from you tomorrow. It may not be the literal tomorrow, but I promise you tomorrow will come, and I want to encourage you to live today like tomorrow is only a day away.

YOUR DAILY WALK IN GRATITUDE

"When you are grateful, fear disappears and abundance appears."
– TONY ROBBINS

In a later chapter I will discuss in detail my morning routine and the importance of creating yours, but for now I want to dive into the time I take every day to be grateful and share with you the incredible benefits!

I start every day in prayer, with a major focus on gratitude for all I have in my life. I try to take the time to remember all the things I take for granted, like freedom, air, my legs, my mind, the fact that I can work, that I can speak, that I can smell . . . the more I remember to be thankful for, the more I appreciate all day every day. (Even if there are things on my list that are no longer on yours, don't get hung up on what you are missing, let's just focus on what we have.)

- **Side Effect 1:** all day I am grateful for the things I would normally take for granted.

- **Side Effect 2:** because I want to add to my list for tomorrow, I am watching for all the things I should be grateful for today.
- **Side Effect 3:** because my day is filled with watching for all that I am grateful for, I don't have the space or energy to spend on things like fear, doubt, regret, and all the other negativity that doesn't serve me.

Take a moment to picture a man walking around all day determined to add to his list of things to be grateful for. If you are like me, you pictured a sweet man with a simple-looking smile on his face. Maybe he is chasing a butterfly or stopping to smell some flowers.

See how he genuinely smiles and greets the stranger who passes? What are his conversations like? I see him fully engaged when you are speaking to him, and he looks like he truly appreciates having the time with you. He looks deep into the eyes of the speaker and thanks them for sharing this moment with him.

Watch how he goes out of his way to thank people for the role they play in his life. I see him encouraging so many people in his day—thanking this person for always bringing a big smile to work, this person for her candles that make everything smell so nice, this guy for his energy that always wakes him up early in the day. I could take all day watching this person in my mind and writing about how awesome his life is.

If you are truly and honestly grateful for every small thing in your life and are daily determined to add to that list, how would you not turn into this person?

CHALLENGE

Take ten minutes today to continue this visualization, but let the main character you are watching be you. Visualize yourself in your normal daily surroundings, but your gratefulness has been turned up to comedically high. Not 10/10, but 58/10. Who are some of the other characters in your story? How do the conversations look? How do you act around other people, your surroundings, the events of the day?

ADVANCED CHALLENGE

Write down your story from above with as much detail as you can muster. Take your story into your day with you (I mean literally—keep it in your pocket all day so you look at it often) and act your story out! Feel free to tone the physical wackiness down so you are more of a 13/10 gratefulness, but keep the essence about you.

At multiple times through the day, write down how interactions went. Did others appreciate you showing your gratitude toward them? How did that make you feel? Did you experience any unique or surprising benefits from the way you acted today? Is it worth trying again tomorrow?

Side Effect 4: instant improvement in every relationship!

I love listening to Lewis Howes. He lives his life with great purpose, and because our mindsets are so well-aligned I find much of what he says to resonate in my life. Here is what Lewis says about gratitude:

> Gratitude is something that we can all practice, regardless of our current situations, and when we focus on being thankful, we become happier as a result.

When we appreciate everything that we already have, it puts us in a mindset of ABUNDANCE rather than scarcity. When we turn our focus off the negative and onto the positive, we call more positive things into our lives. We can then channel that positive energy into everything that we're doing!

And I can't speak for everyone, but gratitude just makes me plain happy! It brings me a ton of joy to pause what I'm doing and give thanks to someone else, or even just in my head. Many of the psychologists I've interviewed on *The School of Greatness* tell me that gratitude is PROVEN to create a happier life.

Here's my suggestion for you: Don't let gratitude be something you just do from time to time or on a holiday. Make it a RITUAL so that you can practice gratitude regularly and bring its full benefit into your life.*

"I am happy because I am grateful. I choose to be grateful. That gratitude allows me to be happy."
– WILL ARNETT

---

* Howes, Lewis. "Gratitude Will Change Your Life." LewisHowes.com/podcast/start-with-gratitude-a-simple-ritual-that-will-change-your-life/.

GRATITUDE = HUMILITY

> "It was pride that turned angels into devils; it is humility that makes men as angels."
> – SAINT AUGUSTINE

Success without humility is not success at all. Have you ever met someone with worldly success (wealth, fine clothing, crazy nice car, etc.), but whose arrogance was so palpable that you couldn't help but imagine they would soon lose it all? Maybe even *hoped* they would lose it all?

Is it really success if everyone is hoping to see you go down? I have found that the opposite also holds true. If you are humble, everyone wants to see you succeed and there are many people who will be happy to go out of their way to assist you in making it happen.

Having a truly grateful disposition will naturally create humility in us. Being truly grateful helps us recognize that as much as you feel like a lone wolf on your journey, it is because of many helping hands you are getting to higher levels in life. The idea of a "self-made man" is a fallacy. This may seem a little contradictory to certain principles I have spoken about in this book, so I will take some extra time to help separate the ideas here.

It will always be your choice, and your choice alone, on how you write your story. It will also be you making billions of decisions to get you to your goals. It will be you alone working countless hours in the shadows as you read, exercise, and build the human who is destined for success.

You will almost certainly have many people in your life who let you down, hold you back, and set you back on your journey; those are the times I know you will feel most alone. But on every step of this journey, you were being catapulted ahead by the teachers, mentors, friends, family, bankers, advisors, cheerleaders, followers, prayer warriors, partners, servers, nurses, doctors, farmers, delivery drivers, internet providers, cooks . . . there always were, and always will be, millions of people doing their part to put you on your path.

If you struggle to recognize that concept, just remember back to Covid times when just one of those groups of people stopped working—remember how fast our whole system came crashing down. Instead of taking all these people (and the million others I neglected to mention) for granted, let's go the other way and take time to think of, and be grateful for, all the people who are making your path straight.

This recognition, this attitude of gratitude, will ooze out of your every pore the more you give into it. People everywhere will recognize it, smell it, feel it and be drawn to it. They won't even necessarily know why, but they will want to see you succeed, and some of them will even go out of their way to improve your life.

This is a great time to remind you that **there are no trophies for the person who "did it themselves."** In fact, every time I hear someone talk about how they are self-made and how they got to where they are with no help, I not only feel sad that they don't see how many people truly did help, but I can't help but ask: Imagine how far you would get if you allowed others to assist and showed some appreciation?

Your support network is working 24/7 whether you recognize it or not. Giving thanks for them, and to them, will not only enhance your life and theirs, but will propel you to your ultimate goal faster, and with more friends to celebrate with you!

CELEBRATING ALL WINS

There is a special amount of dopamine, endorphins, and serotonin released on our brains during celebrations, and I am a huge fan of it! I love how celebrating feels and I encourage everyone around me to look for reasons to rejoice. I kept this expanded section on celebration for the Gratitude principle because the more you celebrate your wins, the more you will be prone to watch and strive for more of them. You increase your gratefulness with each occurrence. Let's start with why being a person who celebrates is an awesome person to be!

I recognized long ago that most people don't take even two seconds to bask in the moment of victory. We are so quick to reach a goal and press on to our next one without skipping a beat. I also discovered that if I step in to highlight that person's achievements and start the celebration for them, people were drawn to me and to the great feelings we created.

We live in a society that focuses heavily on the negative things of this world. Turn on any news broadcast and you will find that in excess of 95 percent of what they discuss is negative and based in fear. This has made the people who subject themselves to the news much more solemn, dark, and susceptible to mental distress and fatigue.

In a recent article published in the *Canadian Medical Association Journal*, Robin Blades states that: **Studies have linked the consumption of bad news to increased distress, anxiety and depression, even when the news in question is relatively mundane.** According to Graham Davey, professor emeritus of psychology at the University of Sussex, exposure to bad news can make personal worries seem worse and even cause "acute stress reactions and some symptoms of post-traumatic stress disorder that can be quite long-lasting."*

Being someone who stops the pity party to bring in some positive noise is like being the guy showing up in the desert with a big glass of water.

I have now become a magnet for great news! Being known as the guy who loves to celebrate the good stuff has people always ready to share the good stuff in their lives with me. You wouldn't believe how much positivity this showers my life with and the positive impact it has had on my relationships and my mental health. And think about how it has positively impacted the mental health of the people bringing me the news. I have inadvertently trained everyone to be watching for good news to share with me because they know I will be the first one jumping for joy. What a beautiful contrast between that state of mind (always watching for positive stuff) and the state the world is trying to put us in (always reporting the negative and scary stuff).

But most importantly, celebrating the wins subconsciously makes your brain work extra hard to create more of them. Releasing the happy hormones on your brain (dopamine, oxytocin, endorphins, and serotonin) not only immediately lights you up, but also creates new pathways in your brain as you start creating plans to succeed more often (I have a positive addiction to these wonderful hormones and I am not afraid to feed it!).

In a 2021 article published in *Development and Learning in*

* Blades, R. "Protecting the Brain Against Bad News." *CMAJ*. 2021 Mar 22;193(12):E428–E429. doi: 10.1503/cmaj.1095928. PMID: 33753370; PMCID: PMC8096381.

Organizations, Swaminathan Mani and Mridula Mishra explain how impactful these hormones are to us:

> Dopamine (mood elevator that enhances happiness and is associated with memory, learning, planning and productivity), Oxytocin (that enhances bonding, trust and empathy), Serotonin (that helps maintain emotional balance and enhances well-being) and Endorphins (boosts self-esteem and reduces anxiety) are all known to enhance productivity, improve collaboration, increase prosocial behavior, reduce stress and boost the overall well-being.[*]

Celebrating every chance I can not only brings me massive pleasure immediately, but it also draws people and positivity to me, and subconsciously creates new paths to more success and celebration.

CHALLENGE

Take ten minutes right now to think of anything you have done in the last three days that deserves celebration. Now celebrate it! I don't care how small you think it is or if you think it is worthy of celebration or not. I also want you to share it with someone close to you and ask if they will celebrate with you. It never hurts to offer that person a beer or dinner or some incentive to "come celebrate with me!"

---

* Mani, Swaminathan and Mishra, Mridula. "Are your employees getting their daily dose of DOSE? A neuroscience perspective to enhance employee engagement."*Development and Learning in Organizations: An International Journal*, Volume 35, Number 5, 2021, pp. 11–14(4). doi: https://doi.org/10.1108/DLO-08-2020-0179.

ADVANCED CHALLENGE

That special someone you shared your success with—ask them about their greatest success in the last few weeks and go overboard in celebrating with them! It might take a little coaxing and coaching from you to help them see the success they had, as they likely breezed right past it. Ask them about a win at work, or in their personal life, at the gym, with their health, with their finances, their sleep, their relationships, anything. Do you see how this one conversation will now change the way they see future successes? And how this whole celebration mindset has changed the way your brain works?

Please tag us with #playabiggergame so we can celebrate with you! (My happy hormones are going to be off the charts when this book comes out and you all start sharing your victories with me!!!)

BEING GRATEFUL FOR YOUR STORY

I have no doubt this principle, for some, will be the most challenging. Learning to be grateful for your story will make a profound difference to your life, your mental well-being, your health, and your relationships. It is also a key part of telling your new story and owning your whole story.

It is easy for us to be grateful for the parts of our story that are good and naturally considered blessings—if you had good parents, health, friends, fun, education, etc. I challenge you to be grateful for the "bad" stuff too.

You are who you are right now because of everything you have been through—everything. Chances are, there is a lot about you that you like. I believe that the people who would be attracted to this book, and furthermore, the people who are still reading this deep into it, are people who already accept, at least to a small degree, that the bad stuff is a critical part of what has shaped them.

I can give you a million clichés about how diamonds are formed under pressure or precious metals being forged in fire, but we all know the simple truth that **struggles build character**.

My life changed dramatically when I learned this lesson. Tony Robbins taught me to "thank my bullies." What an incredible paradigm shift. To recognize, and appreciate, that they had an important role in making me the strong man I am today.

And what a unique conundrum! I don't wish bullying on anyone, especially my children, but without it, where will they develop the toughness that comes from that kind of challenge? That same month I read Malcolm Gladwell's *David and Goliath*, in which Malcolm asks, "You wouldn't wish dyslexia on your child, or would you?" He goes on to explain that kids growing up with dyslexia are forced to work far harder to get ahead, and in many cases it breeds super-high achievers.

I've learned amazing lessons from Tony Robbins.

These two mental powerhouses convinced me that every struggle I had growing up, every challenge, and every situation I saw as failure, pain, and suffering were actually critical building blocks for the man I see in the mirror.

Instead of looking back at my issues as negative and stirring up pain and sadness, I can honestly, and in integrity, look back and smile and be so grateful those building blocks were there. Please take a pause to recognize what a weight that lifted from my life. Those aren't wounds that could easily get ripped back open anymore; they are memories that serve me today.

At that time, those challenges made me feel like I was near the end of my rope and sanity, but look at how they turned me into something awesome. Look at how that removes the fear of future challenges because I know they won't break me; they will only serve me and make me into an even stronger version of me.

Not-So-Fun Story

My bullies were hard on me. As a skinny, extra-tall boy with no self-confidence, I was a walking target everywhere I went. I was picked on by so many groups, even by people who were supposed to be on my side—even players on my own basketball team, whom I spent hundreds and hundreds of hours with. I lived in constant fear.

I remember pulling up to a McDonald's and having the car surrounded by eight guys wanting to harm me. I can still picture the knife I swear I saw one guy partially hiding in his pocket. I remember a girl I liked asking me to hang out at a restaurant after school, only to be warned by a friend that I was going to be jumped by her ex-boyfriend. I did not go.

I could write for hours of the experiences I had that tormented me for many years, but I would prefer to tell you how it positively impacted my story. Because of these events, I am so attuned to bullying that I am the first to stand up to anyone I see picking on someone else. I am extremely sensitive to it and it makes me a more caring, gentle, compassionate man. I stand up for those who can't yet stand up for themselves.

I know these characteristics also make me a far better husband and father. I know these characteristics have helped me stand out and navigate through many business situations as well. They have contributed to the success I experience today. I would not change my story one bit.

I know I am asking a lot of you in turning your past challenges, struggles, trials, pains, and traumas into experiences to be grateful for. I know this won't happen in an instant—it is a journey. I hope I have given you even a taste of how great life can be if you start that journey.

Are you intrigued enough to open your mind to the concept? Are you curious enough to read up further on this principle and build a stronger case for making the same mental shift that I did? If you are, I highly recommend you go get *David and Goliath* by Malcolm Gladwell and *Awaken the Giant Within* by Tony Robbins and read them immediately. The sooner you adopt this mindset, the sooner you will jump onto the fast track to living with far less fear, pain, and emotional baggage, and you can use all that wonderful energy to get ahead in life.

Your story, the story that makes the you of today, is not just made up of rainbows, sunshine, and smiles. **The tough stuff we all have in our past is what builds us tough today. You can't just be grateful for the good stuff—it's a package deal.**

CHALLENGE

Write down three of your story's biggest traumas, challenges, pains, or struggles. Beside each one, write down a positive, empowering characteristic you have today because of that experience. Take a moment to recognize and appreciate that you wouldn't have these wonderful characteristics if you hadn't gone through what you went through.

Think about how those characteristics have served you. Who have you met because you embody those characteristics? Who loves you because of them? Did these characteristics play a role in drawing these people into your life? Is it safe to say these people might not be in your life if you hadn't gone through what you went through? Would you change your story knowing you might lose some key characters?

Looking at this list again tomorrow, and for as many days as you need to look at it, will hopefully soften any pains you associate with your past and start to turn them into peace, grace, and gratitude.

I am so sorry you had to go through what you went through, and I am not trying to make light of it. I have no doubt your struggles were greater than mine and this exercise will be tougher for some than others.

This challenge, and the advanced challenge, will help you on the path to changing your story and creating a better future.

ADVANCED CHALLENGE

Like all other advanced challenges, it is best not to attempt this one until you are able to complete the challenge above. Even more so in this case because this truly is an advanced challenge.

For the next two weeks, I want you to spend time every day being grateful for the experiences you had and the characteristics you now embody. Take time to be grateful for the person you are today, because that person is strong.

You may not understand this yet, but I know you will one day: **you are hundreds of times stronger than you realize.** Every time you recognize how much stronger you are than you were yesterday, also recognize how much stronger you will be tomorrow and live into it.

IMPACTFUL STORY

One of the most remarkable examples of someone grateful for his story is David O'Leary. At nine years old, David was playing with matches and gasoline and it went off like a bomb in his hands. He burned 100 percent of his body, burned down his family home, and was given a 1 percent chance of living. He had to fight harder than most people will ever have to fight, just to stay alive. He lost his fingers, he lost much of his mobility, he lost years of his life, but he didn't lose his will to live.

Now in his mid-forties, David has spoken to and inspired tens of millions of people across the planet. He is a bestselling author. He is a husband and father. David knows he is where he is today, and has in his life all the people in his life today, because of that horrific moment almost forty years ago. David's message is to embrace our own story, both the good and the bad parts.

"1: Our life is a sacred, awesome gift.
2: We get to choose our mindset in every situation, no matter how bleak it seems.
3: Together, we can change the world. Starting with our own."
– DAVID O'LEARY

I WAS KICKED IN THE FACE BY A HORSE

"Trade expectation for appreciation and your whole world changes
in an instant."
– TONY ROBBINS

My inclination was to include this as a "fun" little story somewhere in this book, but the truth is, it has such major ramifications on my life, and envelops so many incredible principles and lessons, I wanted to devote some extra time to it. Let's start with what happened and why **being kicked in the face by a horse was one of the best things to happen to me.**

I was thirteen years old and I was a bit of a prankster (that has no bearing right now, but you'll soon see why I added that). We were at Hills Ranch near 108 Mile in beautiful British Columbia. We were asked to help round up some horses and I was happy to help.

They pointed to a young horse and said, "Be careful with that one, he is a stud and he is pretty crazy." Well since I was hoping to one day be a stud, and fancied myself a little crazy, I went right after that guy! Now before you blame me for this incident, I know not to go near a horse's rear end, I know that.

I went right up to that horse and almost got his bit (the mouth-piece you see horses wearing). Before I could grab it, he took off. I saw him bolt away. But here's where it gets weird and why I know this was meant to be: I turned away from him, almost immediately heard a neigh, turned back toward him and WHAMMO, got booted right in the face! (Of course my memory of timing might have been slightly shaken by the 2,000 lbs. of pressure that had just been released at my chin!)

When I came to, I sat up and felt like I had a mouthful of Chiclets. I spat some of it in my hand and saw a handful of thick red blood, freckled with hundreds of white teeth bits. I got up and looked for help. I covered my mouth (I suppose I was trying to hold my teeth in?) and motioned toward the others.

Since my jaw was pretty rocked and my mouth was full of blood and teeth, I don't know what they heard when I yelled, "I got kicked in the face by a horse!" but everyone started laughing! See, now you get why I mentioned I was a bit of a prankster—they all thought I was joking around! That was until they saw the blood and teeth pouring through my fingers.

You are probably asking why the heck this gruesome story is in the chapter on gratitude! This was a life-changing moment for me in so many ways. I hope my reasoning resonates with you and I hope you see areas in your life where you can apply the same feelings and changes. Without knowing it back then, this was one of the first times in my life I changed my story. I chose to look at the positives instead of focusing on the easy-to-see negatives.

First, before this moment I was quite a crybaby! I cried all the time. I was whiny and it didn't take much to set off the waterworks. I know I didn't like that part of me and honestly, I didn't feel like I was ever going to be a real man with this crying issue. (To be clear, I am not judging others, this was a personal thing. I was crying way too much, about the littlest things. Personally, I was not cool with that.)

When I got kicked that day, I didn't shed a single tear. This was arguably the first time a physical injury really warranted some tears, but I chose to be a man about it. I still remember one of the young, female barn hands attending me as we waited for the ambulance.

"Wow," she said. "I can't believe you aren't crying; you are so tough."

I am so grateful for that moment because it taught me how tough I really was and sealed the lesson with a cute older woman noticing it and complimenting me on it.

Maybe this should have been mentioned first, but I was truly grateful to still be alive and to only have "minimal" injuries. Even if I didn't fully understand it at thirteen, every year that goes by and I think about this story, I recognize that things could have been far worse that day. I was kicked in the face by a young, stud horse. I could have died, had my nose or jaw or cheekbones shattered, he could have got me in the chest or throat . . . there are a million ways that moment could have put me on a completely different path for life or ended my life right there. **I know God had more in store for my life, and because of this moment, I feel like I am on borrowed time; the least I can do is live each moment to the fullest.**

Finally, because of this incident, I have spent hundreds of hours in the dentist's chair. Please note the *s* on the end of *hundreds*. I have had major mouth surgery close to thirty times. I have had root canals, bridges, extractions . . . I don't know if there are many wild dental anomalies that I haven't experienced.

But today, I love my teeth. I am grateful for this reminder. Every time I smile, every time I open my mouth, every time I receive a compliment on my teeth, I am reminded of what could have been and how blessed I am to be here.

I hope you see and believe that none of the positivity toward this incident was forced or fake. My gratitude for this is genuine and has wonderful implications on so many aspects of my life.

Do you think people would understand if I was forever speaking of how hard that day was for me and how it ruined my life? Because of that day I don't try new things, I don't trust animals, I don't smile because my mouth is weird . . . I am confident I could get all the pity I could handle and no one would blame me for allowing that "tragedy" to dictate how my life goes. That victim card is mine to play.

But tell me where the win is in that. Tell me how that story would serve me. Do you have seemingly negative incidents in your life you could turn into positives? Can you learn lessons from them instead of simply saying, "That was my bad luck"? Would you like to trade your victim card in for a victor card?

ADVANCED CHALLENGE

That's right, we are going straight to advanced here because I know this is not going to be an easy one for many of you. I want to encourage you right now commit to doing this challenge in full and do your best to separate the emotion from the incident.

Choose an incident in your life that you see as negative. You are going to answer a huge "what-if" question: What if that incident was meant to happen so you could advance in life? What if this incident was actually a gift for you? What positives came from it? Again, I know many people don't want to suggest there are any positives that came from certain incidents, but I know there are.

Often when I ask this question, the toughest incidents often make people extra sensitive toward others, extra caring, extra supportive, extra loving . . . these are very positive things. Does it make you more appreciative of the people in your life? How about your freedoms, your security, your strength, your ability to understand and be compassionate, the way you can relate to others who share the same afflictions?

I am not asking you (in one five-minute challenge) to start calling your incident a positive experience, but can we at least agree that some positive came from it?

That positive that you are admitting to is YOU. That is YOUR strength. That is how truly incredible you are. The incident that destroyed others completely, it didn't destroy you. Even if you feel destroyed, I am here to tell you that you aren't. If you are reading this book, you clearly have strength and drive in you, and **I know with 100 percent certainty you can make a major impact on the lives of others.**

While my incident may be absolutely nothing compared to yours, I want to encourage you that with time, and with focusing on these positives, you can change your story too. Of course, there were tons of times sitting in the dentist's chair, having the ten thousandth massive needle jammed into my mouth, that I only saw the darkness and wished the whole thing hadn't happened. But here I am today, thankful for it, and all the other crazy crap I have endured to become the man I am. I wouldn't change a thing.

WE ALL HAVE DADDY ISSUES, GET OVER IT!

"You are most powerfully positioned to serve the person you once were."
– RORY VADEN

I wanted to give some space in the book between the story of for-giving my father and this section on daddy issues so you might be in a better place to read this (or maybe I needed some space before I wrote this part—let's not point fingers at each other!). Since I have always had daddy issues, I am extremely sensitive to them. I don't know if I have EVER met someone without daddy issues!

Fathers play such an incredibly impactful role in our lives, whether they are present or absent, loving or horrible, and it leaves a mark on every one of us. I find great comfort in knowing that I am not alone with this issue, and I hope you find solace here too.

A younger, more naïve Markus believed that people with fathers that stuck around couldn't possibly have daddy issues. I also believed that none of their problems could match mine if they had a dad! The truth is, even when people have amazing, loving fathers, daddy issues present in different ways.

Was he too soft on discipline, did he choose your sibling to be his favorite, did he set such high standards that you could never live up to them, was he stingy with his affections? Again, no one I have ever met was safe from their own daddy stories and complications.

If you know, truly believe, and understand that 100 percent of humans deal with daddy issues, does it not help you see that you can move past them too? If others have been able to rewrite their story, and compartmentalize or use their issues as fuel, you can too. **The story you tell yourself about your father that holds you back is truly only a story. You can change your story today and turn this negative into something beautiful.**

My encouragement for you today is to take your daddy issues and be grateful for them. That man had a large part in the person you are today—and that person is amazing! Maybe it will help you to realize your father could have been much worse. Maybe it will help you to use that hurt as fire to push you forward—prove to him and the world that you can be something amazing and he missed out on being a better part of your success.

This is a great chance to stop looking back and start focusing on today and the future. You can't change what happened, but you can decide right now what you will do with it. Will you choose to see it as a 50-pound weight that you carry with you daily, or as the very reason you get out of bed and sprint toward greatness every single morning?

Finally, as my mentor Rory Vaden put it so eloquently, you are the best, most equipped person to help others get over their daddy issues. You have the unique opportunity to help so many others. **Will you step up and be the powerful, life-changing leader you were created to be?** Will you use your backstory as a superpower to heal the world? The choice is yours.

ENCOURAGEMENT

Now that you have developed a greater appreciation for all the amazing things all around you, I want to encourage you to become an encourager! Encouraging someone is one of the most beautiful gifts you can give. Since you are now someone who sees all the good in people and are grateful for the unique qualities and personalities they bring to your life, aren't you the perfect person to give them encouragement for what you see in them?

We live in a world where we rarely receive compliments and encouragement, but are in need of them more than ever. You have now been gifted with the ability and wisdom to fill this incredible void in everyone's life. As I took the "risk" in becoming an encourager (stepping outside my normal comfort zone), I was pleasantly shocked at how it lit people up every time (what other reaction was I expecting?). **It costs me nothing to share that love with the people around me, but the value to the receiver is immense.**

Knowing that I have been gifted with this ability is one of my favorite blessings in my life. I try to encourage someone everywhere I go! You might be thinking it is a ton of work if you haven't started this journey, but imagine being a person who brings that many smiles to the world and fills that many people's buckets every day.

When I encourage someone, I choose the most unique attribute that I like about them. Just offering someone the obvious "you look pretty today" can come off as flattery or, for a married man who wants to stay married, as flirting—really not cool! Telling someone I appreciate their energy, I respect their wild hairstyle, their sick shoes, their deep voice, their great posture, their glow . . .

The best encouragement:

1. **Is accurate:** Don't tell someone you like their energy when their energy is not good.

2. **Is truthful:** If you try to encourage someone on something you don't really care for, trust me, they will know. "I really like your spikey collar and all the tattoos on your face." That's a tough one to sell. (No judgment if you have a spikey collar and tattoos on your face, but I will be honest, I am shocked you are reading this book. If I just described you, please email me. I will be sending you a killer gift—you are a unicorn, my friend, and I dig that!)

3. **Doesn't come across as a flirty compliment:** Unless you want that!

4. **Can't be taken as sarcasm:** "Nice hair" is too vague, and since

everyone is sensitive about their looks, I would say nine out of ten people will think you are making fun of them. Try something more like, "I dig your pink hair—it's bold and confident!"

5. **Is unique to them:** The more unique, the greater the encouragement, and the more you will light up that person's day.

Being an encourager is a beautiful way to live life. You will positively impact so many people, every single day. You will also receive so much encouragement yourself and you will create deeper relationships everywhere you go.

So go, spread that love to the world and claim the positive life that is waiting for you.

"When you encourage others, you in the process are encouraged because you're making a commitment and difference in that person's life. Encouragement really does make a difference."
– ZIG ZIGLAR

DISCIPLINE

Def.

Refers to rule-following behavior, to regulation, order, control, and authority. Discipline is used to create habits, routines, and automatic mechanisms such as blind obedience.

No one was born with great discipline. Therefore, discipline must be learned and mastered like any other skill. As with many characteristics I was missing in my early life, the lack of discipline shined through. I was quick to give up. I was not willing to commit. I would try something with 20 percent effort and assume I was born to be terrible at this thing based on the abysmal results I would see.

I have gone through thousands of sticky notes with quotes and reminders about discipline. I made discipline a main focus in my life because once I had a taste of the success that comes with being disciplined, I became ravenous for more. I realized discipline is 100 percent in my control. Since I have built up my discipline, I now recognize that **mastering this one characteristic alone will result in unbelievable success.**

Take a moment now to think of someone in your life who you consider to be highly disciplined. When you consider their abundance and focus on being disciplined, don't you naturally believe they could accomplish anything if they targeted their discipline at it? Focusing discipline on any given task will result in great success.

My goal for you, by the completion of reading this chapter and powering through every challenge, is for you to consider yourself a disciplined person. Know this, if you read this chapter in full and do the advanced challenges, you will have become a more disciplined person. It is now up to you whether you want to continue being a disciplined being and experience the incredible success that will inevitably accompany your discipline, or choose to go back to your old ways.

SUCCESS STARTS WITH A GOOD NIGHT'S SLEEP

Without a good night's sleep, I am a shell of a man. Yes, I can push through a day or two and still work at a decently high level on a moderate amount of sleep, but remember, we aren't interested in "getting by."

If you want to operate at a champion's level, your systems must be running optimally. Just as lack of good sleep will halt your body's ability to put on muscle and burn fat, it will also hinder your ability to succeed at the level you should be succeeding. It is imperative to get good, healthy, restorative sleep.

Getting good sleep is 100 percent a discipline issue. There are so many ways to get yourself into the right place before bed to optimize your sleep. Just like everything else we have discussed in this book, the world seems to be against us getting that sleep we need, so you will have be mindful of that, and be prepared to go against the masses.

Things that will hinder a good night's sleep (things to cut out at least two hours before bed):

- Looking at your phone
- Any screen time
- Arguing
- Work
- Stressful thoughts
- Politics
- News
- Social media
- Eating anything (but especially bad foods)
- Alcohol and caffeine

Things to enhance your success in bed:

- A calming bedtime routine
- Managing your stress
- Reading before bed
- Prayer
- Exercise during the day
- Healthy eating all day
- Optimal bedroom environment (dark and cool and maybe add some white noise)
- No alcohol in your system
- No food or drinks at least two hours before bed
- A warm and relaxing bath or shower
- A good sleep schedule (going to bed and waking up around the same times each day)
- Avoiding long naps during the day (short naps are encouraged)

It is rare to find any medical institution that doesn't recommend 7–8 hours of sleep for optimal health. I know many successful people who operate with smaller amounts of sleep, but even though they may be able to continue being successful in their business life, their health is taking a back seat and that sleep deficiency will take its toll.

One sleep game-changer for me is keeping a pen and pad of paper next to my bedside for notes. I often have stuff flowing through my mind before bed that I don't want to forget. I used to keep thinking about it, thus ruining my sleep, or I would open my phone to make a note, which turned on that massively disruptive light, which woke my brain up, which ruined my sleep. Having that pen and pad make it easy to quickly jot down the thought, then let it go and clear my mind for sleep.

I highly recommend utilizing a sleep-measuring instrument. I personally use the Oura ring. The Oura ring not only measures and reports my deep, REM, and light sleep, but it also measures my heart rate, latency, restfulness, sleep efficiency, HRV balance, and more.

When things aren't optimal, it gives suggested reasons why (did you have alcohol in your system, too big of a meal, too much screen time . . . ?) and offers recommendations on how to improve it for my next sleep. My favorite thing about the Oura ring is that it allows me to tell a different story.

If I didn't sleep a "perfect" sleep, I used to say "I had a rough night." We have all said that a million times, and when that is the story we tell, how does our day go? It is much harder to have a high-level, high-achieving kind of day when you start your day saying, "I had a rough night and it probably won't be a killer today."

What my Oura ring has taught me is that most nights that I don't think are spectacular sleeps are actually still very good (like an A- kind of good). A "really bad" sleep for me usually measures around a B or B-. I am confident I can still have an excellent day, even if I started out with only a B- sleep!

For me personally, this has equated to roughly forty-five days per year that I used to write off that I now dominate. I just added forty-five amazing days to my year! **Would you be more successful with forty-five bonus amazing days each year of your life?**

This all comes back to writing your own story. If you do the right things before bed, prepare your mind for a great sleep, and read the measurements that suggest you are ready for a great day, it seems like a forgone conclusion to me how your day will go—you will dominate it!

I have one last big picture idea I want to give you about sleep, and why I want you to make a good night's sleep a top priority in your life. Not only will you receive all the benefits I have mentioned and be set up for high-level success, but by making sleep a key focus in your life, you will automatically create and implement many other disciplines I have outlined in this book to make it happen.

You will need daily exercise, you will need to eat better, watch less TV, do less screen time, less social media, less news, manage stress better, create better relationships, read more, drink less, remove negativity, and much more. By making sleep a top priority, you will be giving yourself extra reasons, and writing better files, for the importance of all these other principles you are hoping to make your default daily rituals.

One of the greatest basketball players of all time, LeBron James, consistently credits his sleep for his energy and performance. It has naturally become the main topic of numerous interviews he has given. When talking about sleep with Tim Ferris, LeBron explains, "[sleep is] the best way for your body to physically and emotionally be able to recover and get back to 100 percent." He goes on to explain that with a good night's sleep, "**I can tackle this day at the highest level.**"

That is exactly what we are trying to do—set ourselves up for the greatest likelihood of success. If we can't tackle this day at the highest level, we are missing numerous opportunities to get ahead.

In a recent interview, Dr. W. Christopher Winter, MD—the president of Charlottesville Neurology and Sleep Medicine and CNSM Consulting—said, "**Sleep is the most important thing in the world for an athlete.**"

You may not yet consider yourself an athlete, but as we strive to be a greater version of ourselves, we need to watch for every opportunity to get ahead, to optimize our life, and to learn from the people doing it best.

Sweet dreams, my friend.

IMPORTANCE OF A MORNING ROUTINE

Your morning sets the tone for the entire day. I have found great success in having a strong morning routine and having everything planned out the night before. I am confident you will agree that first thing in the morning is not the best time to be making decisions.

At night, before bed, I love laying out my workout clothes, choosing my work outfit, laying out my morning supplements, and setting up my breakfast. In the morning, I stumble downstairs half-asleep, take my supps, get my cardio clothes on, and get on my treadmill within six minutes of waking. I am a huge fan of morning, fasted cardio (that means cardio before I eat breakfast). Thousands of studies have proven the millions of benefits morning cardio offers, but I will focus on the benefits for my life.

Morning cardio gets my blood flowing and wakes me up. I do twenty-five to forty minutes, five times per week, walking briskly on a steep incline on my treadmill. I spend the first fifteen minutes in prayer. What a perfect way to start my day—getting my body moving and speaking with my creator. I spend a good chunk of my prayer time in gratitude.

Starting my day by thinking of all the things I am grateful for puts me in an exceptional mood and keeps me watching all day for things to be thankful for tomorrow morning. **If I fill my mind with gratitude, there is no space to think of all the negative in the world around me.**

I also spend a fair amount of my prayer time asking for forgiveness. This repentance has a beautiful effect on my days. If I know I need to repent my sins every day and come to my Lord asking to be forgiven, I spend more time in my day avoiding sin and temptations because I don't want to bring them up the next morning.

After prayer, I start thinking about all the ways I can have a successful day. I intentionally focus away from anything negative that might pop into my head and stay focused on the positive. I like to think about possible business moves, how I will treat the people around me, how I can serve someone today, how I will treat my family, what my next workout will look like . . . I keep my mind focused on how this will be a powerful, impactful day.

When I have a speaking engagement coming up, I use my extra time on the treadmill to practice my talk over and over. This practice gives me so much confidence, as well as tons of extra time to tweak and improve my talks. I usually practice any given speech over a hundred times in full.

So far I have set my morning up to avoid temptations and the bad stuff in life, while watching for all the great stuff I can be thankful for. Does this not sound like a nearly flawless recipe for a great day? Add to it that I got my body moving, my blood flowing, my mind sharp, and have already completed a workout . . . and I haven't even been up for an hour yet!

After my fasted cardio, I take 10–15 minutes to stretch. Stretching keeps my body loose, further improves blood flow and circulation, prevents injury, allows my body to perform better all day, and improves my sleep at night.

At 6'6", I am far more likely to have back issues than someone of average height, and I take that risk seriously. I know that my 8–10 hours in front of a computer each day only increase my likelihood of back pain. My stretching, exercise, and healthy lifestyle have kept me pain free for virtually my whole adult life.

I then eat my usual breakfast, which contains 1 cup of slow oats (microwave these first) plus 1.5 scoops of Magnum Quattro protein powder (or 1 cup of egg whites), 1 tbsp. organic coconut oil, and 1 cup of blueberries. This breakfast is perfectly balanced for me. It gives me clean protein sources, healthy, slow digesting carbohydrates, essential fats, and some vitamins and antioxidants. This is easy on digestion and gives me steady energy for hours.

At this point I have not yet opened any emails, texts, social media, or news. Far more often than not (almost flawlessly), these will send you on a negative path for the day. The purpose is to keep you clear from any possible negative exposure.

That is my daily morning routine. I would say 364 days per year look almost exactly the same (maybe once per year I order room service to celebrate an anniversary or special occasion with my family).

The benefits of my morning routine:

- Great focus all day
- High energy all day
- A focus on the positive while blocking out the negative
- Entering the world with a spirit of gratitude
- An injury-free, healthy body
- A focus on serving God and serving others
- A clear conscience for great sleep
- Great sleep!

CHALLENGE

For the next three days, create and execute a consistent morning routine. Remember that a great morning routine starts the night before. Lay out your cardio clothes and choose your power outfit for your workday.

If you don't have a treadmill, go for a power walk outside. Spend time in gratitude, and focus on how your day will be positive and impactful. If your mind wanders toward anything remotely negative, corral it back to the positive. Remember to stay off email, text, social media, and news in your morning.

I know some of you live in a cold climate and walking outside sounds like a nightmare. I encourage you to look for a used tread-mill online. For decades I used $200 to $250 used treadmills for this morning routine. The value this purchase brought me was immea-surable (but certainly far higher than $250!).

ADVANCED CHALLENGE

Make it a full fourteen days! If you take on this advanced challenge, it is going to be hard for you to unlearn what you just learned. You will feel far more positive every day. You will have more energy and focus, and you will feel accomplished by the time you get to work! The biggest question will be: Why would you want to go back to your old ways?

Tag our community with #playabiggergame and show us the success you are experiencing in the mornings. Allow us to cheer you on and keep you going!

GETTING YOUR EXERCISE

"No citizen has a right to be an amateur in the matter of physical training . . . what a disgrace it is for a man to grow old without ever seeing the beauty and strength of which his body is capable."
– SOCRATES

If you know me, you are probably shocked I haven't already written twenty pages about working out! Getting a proper amount of exercise does far more for your life than just help you get the body you desire. **If you want to have true success in life, it can't be done without your health.** What good is all the money in the world if your health is falling apart? It saddens me deeply to know that somehow, over time, exercise and health became two separate concepts.

Myth: Exercise drains our energy.

Truth: Exercise produces energy for the whole day and allows us to operate at a higher level, both physically and mentally.

It's time you wrote a new story about exercise.

If you have always found exercise to be draining, mind-numbing, and dreadful, you simply haven't found the right exercise for you. Can you imagine someone not liking lawn bowling and saying, "I hate all sports?" Sounds ridiculous, right? Handing them a basketball or soccer ball might change that person's life by adding thousands of hours of enjoyment, community, friendship, exercise, passion . . . but if they have closed their mind off to all sports, all those positive benefits will be forever missed out on. It is imperative that you continue to try all forms of exercise until you find the one that suits you. The right exercise is life-giving.

If you are someone who struggles with having an exercise routine, it is likely you need to start with rewriting the file you have on exercise. It is likely you are still operating on an old file that is telling you that exercise sucks and the reason for exercise in anyone's life is of little value to you.

Fun Story

I'd like to share with you why exercise will never be a chore for me, but a great honor and privilege.

You already know that I grew up with a flimsy, embarrassing physique! Standing 6'4", at a whopping one hundred and twenty pounds soaking wet, I heard thousands of comments about how bad I looked.

What led me to my first workouts I can only say was divine intervention. It only took a few for me to feel better about myself. Just doing something about your problem, anything, helps you feel like you are in control, even if it is only a small amount of control.

I liked how I felt, and I gained confidence and self-worth overnight. My body hadn't even changed a tiny bit, but that didn't matter. People looked at me differently. People treated me differently. I saw these as massive wins and that got me pushing even harder and committing more to the gym. Now people started showing me respect for the fact that I was going. Again, they weren't respecting me for having a nicer body or any of the normal reasons people think we go to the gym, but just for going at all!

It wasn't long before I was feeling stronger. I was lifting slightly more weight and that turned into more confidence outside the weight room too. I was a basketball player at that time in my life, and not a good one!

Most embarrassingly, at 6'4" I was barely able to grab the rim (for those of you who don't know, grabbing the rim/dunking/jumping high is everything to a fifteen-year-old baller!). Since my legs were getting stronger and my confidence was increasing, I started jumping higher and higher and higher. By the start of the twelfth-grade basketball season, I was dunking like a champ! Reverses, alley-oops, windmills—I was the warm-up show! People were now cheering for me and impressed with what my body could do.

So let me frame this in a different way for you—I went from being made fun of daily for my embarrassing physique and lack of physical ability to having crowds of hundreds of people cheering for me for my physical prowess! What changed? I started working out. I will never feel like I HAVE to workout or drag myself to the gym—I GET to workout and it is a privilege to train.

It has been almost thirty years since I changed my story and not once in those thirty years have I questioned if the gym is still right for me or if I need exercise in my life.

As with rewriting any old file you have in your mind, you will need to be prepared to be patient and follow all the guidelines we have discussed.

Steps to rewriting your old exercise file:

1. Recognize and accept that your current view of exercise isn't serving you and that it does in fact need to be replaced.

2. Recognize and accept the mass amount of benefits exercise will have in your life. (If you don't see all the value as I have outlined above, take fifteen more minutes to read about it from other authors you respect—more energy, more confidence, look better in clothes, look better out of clothes, sleep better, less aches and pains, less illness, more community, more outdoor activities, better health for your family . . .)

3. Write down the cost of not exercising (illness, weight gain, poor sleep, lack of confidence, lack of energy, higher stress, impotency . . .)

4. Write down all the reasons you will enjoy the journey.

5. Take time to recognize the benefits of step 4 as they arise to further solidify that you were right about this process.

6. Every thirty to sixty days, repeat steps 1–5 to make sure your file is perfectly updated and relevant.

Ultimately, we are trying to create this new file in a way that exercise just naturally becomes part of your default routine. Often people ask me how I stay motivated to consistently get to the gym year after year. I ask them in return how they stay motivated to consistently brush their teeth every day, year after year. Brushing your teeth has nothing to do with motivation. You don't skip brushing your teeth because you are having an off day or don't have the energy for it.

Somehow you created a file that brushing your teeth must happen every single day, no matter what. We simply need to create your exercise file in the same way.

We need to establish that this is our new identity and filter all decisions through it. Should I skip my workout today? No, I am a healthy person who exercises. Should I go have fast food for lunch? No, I am a healthy person who eats right.

Far too often our new fitness goals are overpowered by a negative identity trait that we have held onto for years and give far too much power over our lives. Do any of these comments sound familiar:

"I'm cheating on my diet—that is so me."

"I didn't even last a week in the gym—I always give up."

We wear these negative identity traits like a badge of honor! It's time to catch ourselves and use empowering words that suit our new identity.

Let's take a deeper dive into the six points above and write your new exercise file together.

1: Recognizing that your current file must be replaced

Until you believe and accept that the file is wrong and needs to be updated, you won't be able to. Until you recognize something is broken, your mind will not be focused on fixing it. Steps 2–4 will assist you in your realization that there is a better file to have on exercise.

2: Recognizing the benefits

With brushing your teeth, you were likely taught two things: the positive effects of brushing your teeth (pretty smile, whiter teeth, fresh breath, more kissable mouth . . .) and the negative impact of not brushing (which we will tackle next). Now let's create the same benefits list for exercise:

Positives

- Better energy all day
- Better focus
- Better sleep
- Better mood
- Better sex life
- Healthier skin
- Less stress and anxiety
- Reduced pain
- More strength
- Healthier immune system
- Better smell
- More confidence
- More friends (both because you are now more awesome and because of the relationships in the gym you will naturally create!)
- Better body
- Better fit in clothes
- More attractive to potential suitors (or your spouse!)
- Less time at the doctor and hospital
- Less drain on the health care system
- Better influence on the next generation
- Longer life

These are just some of the benefits. Please make your own list and add as many of the benefits as you can that have value to you.

3: Recognizing the costs of not exercising

As I am confident you learned with brushing your teeth, there is a cost to not brushing (gum disease, infections, messed-up smile, bad breath, discolored teeth, repulsion for suitable kissers . . .). Now let's make a list of the costs of not exercising:

- Low energy
- Low confidence
- More time at the doctor
- More time in the hospital
- More health issues (heartburn, high cholesterol, indigestion, gut issues, skin issues . . .)
- More likely to get serious illnesses (diabetes, heart disease, stroke, cancers, brain issues . . .)

Honestly, I am uncomfortable filling the rest of this list in, but I would like you to. I feel like people will think I am coming down on them or judging people who don't exercise, and that is not at all what this is about. You need to make this list for yourself, so you know all the pitfalls of avoiding exercise. Make exercise and teeth brushing the same file in your head so you will do both daily without needing pep talks or motivation.

4: Enjoying the journey

As you start on your fitness journey, I would like you to focus not just on the end goal (having a better body), but on the journey itself. Focus on the energy you are getting from the exercise each day. Focus on the great sleep you are having because of it, the way your digestive system is improving, how you don't feel as heavy as often, how you aren't getting sick as often, and the way your mind has more energy and clarity all day.

Maybe you want to focus on how you are feeling and looking younger, and on your improved sex drive. You can focus on how you have more to discuss with the fit and healthy people at work.

What's most important about these benefits is that they have value to you and that you are driven by the things you are noticing.

5: Recognizing and celebrating the wins

As you see the results we discussed in step 4 coming true in your life (and some of those results will come quickly), take the time to sit, ponder, and celebrate these results. Think of it like building a case you are presenting in court.

The opposition has been working for years building their case and greasing the judges with bacon cheeseburgers, sleeping in, binge watching shows, and twelve-packs of beer. So every time you get the good feelings from your new routine, you need to write them down and make sure your brain is ready to present the evidence that this new lifestyle is better. Every good sleep, every feeling of accomplishment, all the good soreness from working out, less back pain, more sex drive, more energy, more confidence . . . this is hard evidence that you, the jury, must look at, analyze, and believe beyond a shadow of a doubt so you can stay on this high-achieving path and not fall back into routines that will only hold you back in life.

6: Repeating steps 1–5 for accuracy and relevancy

Do you recall the story I told you earlier in the book about the compliment I received for almost twenty years that I saw as a bit of an insult? I didn't accept being called athletically muscular because I wasn't regularly updating my files. The file you create early in your exercise journey will almost certainly not stay relevant for more than a few months, so updating it regularly will keep you motivated and focused.

Fun Story

My big brother Darren has recently rewritten his exercise file and has dramatically changed his physique and his life. He was fifty-three years old when he chose to update his file. Here is what my big bro had to say about his rewrite:

> Since I coach this stuff, I finally decided it was time to change my story on health earlier this year. My whole life, exercise hasn't really been a thing. When I was younger, sports kept me in good shape. But as I aged, the sports stopped. I got out of shape. I've been carrying an extra 20–30 lbs. on me for a few decades. Along the way, I've had small stints of exercise. Go to the gym for a while, do some hikes, walk the golf course here and there. But I really didn't have much drive for more. Excuses included (but were not limited to) I'm injured/sore, it doesn't matter/ who cares, I'm too old, I don't have the time/energy.
>
> This year (2022), I started looking at my life through a different lens. I wanted to live all my life through my biggest value—integrity. As I looked at my body, I was out of integrity. I approached the subject of getting into the best physical shape of my life the way I would coach a client to. Why is it a big want? Who is going to support you? What is the plan? Is it realistic? What habits do you need to break, what habits do you need to create?
>
> Want: I can't be in integrity and lead others in this way if I am lying to myself that this is okay.

Support: My little brother. Been there, does it every day!

Plan: Gym plan. Four to five times a week until it's a lifestyle. After six weeks straight, reward myself by hiring a trainer. Food plan. Get clear on what I'm taking in and what I need to give myself the best chance of success.

Habits: Old ones need breaking. No energy—track it . . . is that true? Injuries—can I workout anyways?

New: The gym—make it fun.

Food: Get educated. More protein, less junk.

Happy to report that the healthy lifestyle is now what I'm living. I go to the gym at least five times a week. It's one of my favorite places to go. I have a community there. I'm lifting more, doing more. It's scheduled in. I don't miss. I have more energy and vitality than ever. My body is looking better (still a work in progress). My food intake has gone . . . up. Way up. Instead of fasting and fighting, I'm nourishing properly. Basically eating differently and full all the time.

Sleep is way better. Business is better. Mental sharpness way up.

I can't even begin to tell you how proud I am of my big brother. I daily get compliments and reports from the people in the gym at how awesome my brother is doing and how much everyone loves him. Had he not made the choice to change his story, he would have missed out on so much energy, life, friendship, integrity, encouragement, and maybe even this newfound relationship with his younger brother.

My brother Darren's transformation over nearly a year. The top photo (with our sister, Karen Fox, in the middle) was taken Christmas 2021. The bottom photo is from November 2022. Darren lost a lot of weight and also gained more than ten pounds of muscle.

FUELING YOUR BODY

"You can't out-train a bad diet."
-EVERYONE WHO EVER TOOK EXERCISE
SERIOUSLY!

Without creating a better relationship with food, you will never reach your potential physically or mentally. Since I have been in the fitness industry for over twenty-five years and have helped countless people achieve their fitness and body goals, assisted in the loss of over three million pounds of fat worldwide, and reached my own personal physical goals (after decades of failing at it), I hope you will take what I am about to say as hard fact: **how your body looks is 10 percent exercise and 90 percent diet.**

Remember in school when an exam was worth 90 percent of the grade? You could absolutely kill it all year, but if you bomb the final, you were going nowhere. So it is with the food you consume. **No matter how hard you exercise, how committed you are to the gym and getting your sweat on, you will have nowhere near your best physical or mental capabilities without getting the diet right.**

This isn't about being perfect. I am not going to be a killjoy and take away all the foods you love. I love food; I would even argue I enjoy food more than the average person. Here's why: Who do you think enjoys a hamburger more—the person who eats three of them each week, or the person who eats one every three months but looks forward to it and dreams about it for the weeks leading up to it?

The fuel we put in our bodies not only changes how our bodies look, but far more importantly, changes how our minds and bodies feel and operate. How can we expect to be high achievers and get far ahead of the pack when we are constantly feeling weighed down, sluggish, foggy, low energy, tired, gassy, constipated, diarrheal (for any *Office* fans out there, I have always wanted to naturally infuse that word into my writing)?

Now that I have explained the importance of fueling our bodies right, I will give you a few tips on how to reset how you look at food to help shift your mindset and set you up for success.

I will also mention that yes, this will require discipline in staying on track, but I want that discipline focused always on the benefits of clean eating and how it is critical to you becoming the person you were called to be.

This is not about "willpower." I don't have a nice way to say this, but *willpower* is a word used by weak people when giving themselves carte blanche at the food trough. What you are doing is something far better and stronger. It is telling a new story about what food is and does.

If you look at our society and don't see a health problem, I honestly don't know how much help I am going to be to you. I have to assume that by reading this book, you recognize all the problems with physical and mental health in our society and want something better for your life.

As with virtually every principle in this book, we need to give you a new story about food. It will help to recognize what your current story is. Maybe at a young age you were taught that food was a prize for working hard. Maybe you were taught that food is all the same, just eat up. At some point you created a story, a file, about food, that is no longer serving you, so let's update it.

I will share with you my story. I hope you like pieces or all of it and want to adopt it as your story too. **Food is the fuel that allows my mind and body to do truly spectacular things every day.** If the foods that I am considering consuming do not fit into that story, they are considered treat foods. Treat foods can only be consumed during designated treat meals.

Boom. That is my full story. If you can make this your story too, your life, body, mind, energy, focus, sex appeal, sex drive, strength, discipline, and confidence will be forever changed. Interested in getting there?

I would be shocked if you weren't right now thinking, "Markus, that sounds easy enough, but I have tried diet after diet and failed too many times to think it is that easy." This time will be different if you choose to start with being confident in your new story, a story that begins, "This time it was different!"

My principle of baby steps is the best place to start. This would be a great time to go back to the section on baby steps in Principle 2: Choice, and reread it. Today you are going to start with a few small changes to what you eat. You are NOT going to try to do a full overhaul overnight.

Baby steps, when it comes to diet, is making one or two small, positive changes to your meals for the next few days. The challenges I set out in the baby steps section are the best place to start in making these changes.

I also want to change how you speak to your food! I have witnessed, on far too many occasions, people saying the exact opposite things they should be saying when consuming food. If you are about to eat a piece of cake and say to yourself, "This cake is going to make me fat," guess what your brain tells your body to do with that cake?

"Make this fat."

When you eat clean food, if you say, "This is going to be boring and gross," guess how it is about to taste. When I eat a treat, which I only eat when I have decided I need it, I say, "My body needs this cake! My muscles are craving it and they will suck it right up!" When I eat clean food, I say, "This food is going to give me so much energy, strength, and focus, and I am going to love how I feel eating it."

If you use my words, your world will change. You will be getting your brain on your team, as opposed to setting yourself up for guaranteed failure.

But before the above talk can work properly, it must be true and align with your integrity. That means it won't work if you eat cake every day and try to trick your body into thinking it needs it—it doesn't. That means it won't work when you eat dry, boring, gross-tasting health food and try to trick your brain into thinking it's tasty—it won't work.

These points will come up if you revert back to your old stories. One story many people have created is that healthy food has to be boring and gross—that simply isn't true, but if you make it true by trying to eat boiled chicken and plain rice, I assure you it will become true. You won't last more than forty-eight hours—I know I wouldn't.

One of the easiest ways to make healthy food delicious is to find a no-calorie sauce that you love—and use it always! I love Frank's Red Hot Sauce and their Buffalo Wings Sauce. I switch between the two and sometimes add mustard, which is also very low calorie. I never get tired of these flavors. I add sauce to chicken, rice, turkey, meats . . . I get to eat healthy foods and enjoy them too!

It may take some time for you to find sauces you enjoy, so have fun with the process. Try mixing two or three of them together to make your own unique blend, but remember, they must be either calorie free or under four calories per tablespoon, otherwise you are adding mounds of sugar and it isn't healthy anymore.

Finally, constantly remind yourself, and put up sticky notes everywhere, to keep it front of mind why you are doing this. **Fueling your body correctly is a non-negotiable if you want to be a true high achiever and experience real, long-lasting success in all aspects of life.**

Key steps in changing the way you view food:

1. Change your story
2. Baby steps
3. Fix the way you speak to food
4. Find a low or no-calorie sauce you love
5. Recognize and take note of all the positive changes

Fun Story: How my commitment to clean eating caught the attention of my soul mate!

I met Brooke at church during a young-adults event. I was seated in the main sanctuary, hanging with my friends, when this absolute stunner came out of nowhere! I immediately asked someone to introduce us. I kept chitchatting and gave just enough to make her curious about me.

Later in the night, I snuck into the back rows, far from the crowds, to open my cooler and have a meal. Brooke "happened" to be strolling past (come on, we both know she was looking for a 6'6" Lithuanian!), saw me eating something, and inquired, "Is that ice cream?" I showed her the chicken breast I had on my fork and we laughed and laughed!

As Brooke tells the story today (my favorite story that she tells by the way), she talks about how bizarre it was for a young guy to remove himself from the fun to go sit in a dark, quiet place to eat chicken, and how she was drawn in, "This guy must have an incredible story." My passion and commitment to my health has given me a billion benefits, but none compared to it catching the eye of my bride.

GOOD PROTEINS	BAD PROTEINS
Chicken	Pork (feel free to argue on this one, but I don't know if any of my healthy community keeps pork in their regular diet)
Fish	Fatty meats
Lean Meats	
Turkey	
Magnum Quattro (protein powder)	
Eggs	
Egg Whites	

GOOD CARBS	BAD CARBS
Quinoa	White rice
Slow rolled oats	Pasta
Brown rice	Chips
Sweet potatoes	Pop
Yams	Candy
Lentils	Sugar
	Cereal
	Most sauces and salad dressings
	Virtually all desserts
	Crackers
	Cookies
	Fries
	Bread and bagels

GOOD FATS	BAD FATS
Avocado	Butter
Organic virgin coconut oil	Creams
Egg yolks	Margarine
(IMPORTANT: good fats are only good in moderation!)	Shortening
	Sour Cream
	Ice Cream
	Pastries
	Doughnuts
	Muffins
	Anything fried
	Most peanut butters
	And pretty much any fats not listed on the good fats!

Items from the good column should always be your focus and should make up over 95 percent of your consumption (that is nineteen out of twenty meals). That will be your goal, but don't try to get there by tomorrow. Baby steps.

The foods in the bad column will be reserved for your treat meals.

As a sample of a clean diet, combine any of the good proteins with good carbs and good fats and aim for approximately thirty to forty grams protein, thirty to forty grams carbs, and five to fifteen grams fat per meal, four to five meals per day (this is based on an active, 180-pound male).

There are many variables to consider though, including your weight, height, age, activity level, how many meals you are eating per day, and more. If you are serious about making this change, I have many coaches in my inner circle I would be happy to introduce you to who will create a perfect plan for you. Just reach out to me and I can put you in touch.

TWO FINAL FOOD TIPS TO CHANGE YOUR LIFE: DRINK MORE WATER. EAT MORE BROCCOLI!

Short version: almost no one drinks enough water. We need water for everything we do. Every organ, every cell, every muscle depends on water to survive (and thrive). Did you know that dehydration is often mistaken for hunger? Without hydrating properly, you might reach for more food, even though all your body wanted was a light, non-calorie beverage!

Broccoli is God's green gift to us! This green goodness has loads of health benefits, but what I want to focus on is how it keeps us regular and satiated (you won't feel hungry as often and won't succumb to snacking and overeating).

You know those massive bags of broccoli crowns they sell at Costco and most grocery stores? When I am at my peak physical and mental state, I am eating one of those bags every two days. So whatever amount of broccoli you are consuming, you can consume more!

Pro tip: don't eat it raw! Raw means you likely add salad dressing to get it down, which adds loads of empty, useless calories and defeats the purpose. Plus, raw broccoli gives almost every human uncomfortable gas. I blanch my broccoli (boil water, then add the broccoli and bring the water back to boil, then strain and eat). This is easier to chew, tastes better, and is way easier on the digestive system. Enjoy.

FIVE SUPPLEMENTS EVERYONE SHOULD TAKE

Supplements are products designed with various benefits, like improving your health, focus, energy, immune system, sex drive, gut health, memory, and strength. They can help you reach your goals faster, but also help you enjoy the journey more too. Before I offer some tips on supplements I believe everyone should take, I want to make sure you understand this: these are supplements—they are made to supplement your diet, not replace anything.

1: A Multivitamin/Multimineral

In the same way you lay a base of primer before you paint, a great multi is a base for your health. If you don't have the bare minimum requirements, it will be hard to put on muscle, burn fat, sleep right, have the right energy, etc. Key elements you want to find in a multi are vitamins, minerals, antioxidants, essential fats, brain support, digestive support, amino acids—all the essentials to prime you for high-achievement. These ingredients will also boost and keep your immune system strong so you reduce downtime caused by illness.

Suggested product: Magnum Primer

2: Greens

How many of us get our vegetable servings in every day? Yes, I said *servings* with an *s*. And no, I am not talking about products like ketchup and pizza that the government has somehow deemed to be vegetables (and we wonder why obesity is running rampant).

Even if you tell me you get multiple, clean vegetable servings EVERY day, have you seen a study comparing vegetable nutritional value today compared to the nutritional value of vegetables in our grandparents' day? Because of many reasons like pollution, over-farming and soil depletion, even if we get our servings in, we aren't getting all we need from them. A greens supplement is vital to your health.

In choosing a greens supplement, you want it to be 100 percent all natural, loaded with organic greens, and tasting good (or you won't drink it daily)!

Getting my serving each day helps me cleanse and detox, helps me stay focused with level energy, lowers my stress and anxiety, boosts my immune system, keeps me looking and feeling young . . . do I really need to keep going? Finally, as a mindset bonus, it feels right to get my veggie servings in and I know that I am helping my health by doing it.

Suggested product: BioEdge Greens Complex

3: Nootropic

A nootropic is a supplement for the brain. The main ingredients in great nootropics have been clinically proven to give you clarity and focus, improve memory and mental energy, while reducing brain fog and anxiety. **A nootropic will help you think more clearly and maximize your brain's potential**—sounds like something every reader of this book is looking for!

Suggested product: Magnum Mane Brain

4: Gut Health/Probiotics

It feels like every day we are hearing about new gut illnesses or new problems associated with a problem gut. It is rare to find anyone anymore who boasts of having an iron gut and who doesn't, at some point or another, deal with gas, bloating, discomfort, or indigestion. In choosing a good gut health product, you want to look for pre- and probiotics, as well as known herbal extracts that enhance good gut bacteria and help you avoid all the issues associated with bad gut bacteria.

Suggested product: BioEdge Gut Health

5: Protein Isolate

Without enough clean protein in our diet, we can't function optimally. A protein deficiency will cause low energy, fatigue, muscle strain and stress, aches, weight and water gain, lack of recovery, and almost no chance for muscle gain. It is important to have a clean protein supplement daily to meet our protein requirements, without preparing and eating food 24/7. I focus exclusively on isolate proteins—these are proteins that are lactose free, gluten free, low in carbs and fat, and won't cause gas.

Suggested Product: Magnum Quattro

By adding these supplements to your daily routine, you are optimizing your mind and body to produce the way you need it to produce.

You must be disciplined in taking your chosen supplements every day. **If you know you could be 10–20 percent more effective today by taking your supplements, why would you ever choose to not take them?** Set alarms, write sticky notes, put the supplements in your pockets—whatever you need to do to never miss your dose.

Remember that not all supplements are created equal. I choose for my body, and exclusively recommend, products from companies that focus on integrity and are in this world to make it a better place for all of us. Both Magnum and BioEdge are companies with real focus on their WHY—they are here to help others, improve our lives, and serve. I have never found companies in the health and supplement space that gave back more to their communities, and to the world, than these two companies do. And yes, it just so happens I sit on the board of both!

EXERCISE FOR YOUR MIND AND FOR VICTORY

"The body is very important, but the mind is more important than the body."
– ARNOLD SCHWARZENEGGER

This is an advanced mindset concept. Exercise gives more benefits than everything we have already discussed. **The benefits to the mind might be the top benefits I receive from exercise.** Every single workout I get to experience great victories. While yes, my life has many victories every day, I don't take a single one for granted. I suspect many of you reading this would love to have more victories in your life.

Every time I workout I have the choice to stay home and rest, play, goof off, or watch TV, but I choose to workout and that is a small victory in itself. I know that every time I choose to workout, I am among the 1 percent of 1 percent of 1 percent of humanity that is going to exercise that day, and that is a major victory.

When I am exercising, I am pushing myself to be 1 percent better than yesterday and that push is a victory in itself. Finally, when I complete my workout, not only have I done what most people on this planet are not willing to do, not only did I discover new strength (both mentally and physically), but I have now boosted my energy for the whole day, I am closer to my dream physique, and I have earned the food I will eat all day and not feel guilty consuming it. Does this not sound like a champion's mindset?

Fun Story

I used to be heavily into spin classes. Spin classes, in case you don't know, are exercise classes with these unique stationary bikes that are set up in rows, facing the instructor. The instructor blasts motivational, high-BPM tunes and yells at you for around an hour straight! You turn the tension higher and lower throughout, do some standing riding, seated, chest-up, chest-down, side-to-side, trying to simulate a hard ride through mountains and valleys. Ultimately, spin class is just you against yourself because no one knows how hard you are pushing compared to anyone else—but you know.

As always, my goal was to simply push harder than I did the day before. I would leave these classes absolutely drenched; that was a key signal that I had given it my all and could walk away feeling accomplished.

One particular class, I remember pushing on a crazy new level. I was riding like a man possessed. Every time I thought I had reached my limit, I pushed even harder and for longer than ever before. When the class was over, I had never felt that deep a sense of accomplishment. As I looked over my soaked body, I noticed my shorts were soaked as though I had jumped into a pool. Had I worked so hard that I peed my pants? Instead of feeling embarrassed about it, I felt the greatest sense of accomplishment: I could train so hard that I legitimately didn't know if I had lost control of my bladder.

If I want to be a top dog in this world, I must be willing to push harder than everyone else. On that day, I proved to myself how hard I was willing to push.

There are few people on this planet who train their body and mind as hard as David Goggins. He is often recognized as the "toughest man in the world." Not only was he in the US Air Force and Navy SEALs, he did the Army Ranger training "just for fun," and then went on to become an ultra-marathoner (many of these runs requiring over one hundred miles in twenty-four hours) and compete for multiple physical world records!

His book *Can't Hurt Me* is a must read (through I personally recommend the "clean" version—I'm not big on swearing, as you might have noticed). When it comes to body and mind training and strength, Goggins has many incredible nuggets of wisdom, so I added a few below to get you fired up!

"I loved waking up at 5 a.m. and starting work with three hours of cardio already in the bank while most of my teammates hadn't even finished their coffee. It gave me a mental edge, a better sense of self-awareness, and a ton of self-confidence, which made me a better SEAL instructor. That's what getting up at the a** crack of dawn and putting out will do for you. It makes you better in all facets of your life."

"Physical challenges strengthen my mind so I'm ready for whatever life throws at me, and it will do the same for you."

"Only you can master your mind, which is what it takes to live a
bold life filled with accomplishments most people consider beyond
their capacity."
– DAVID GOGGINS*

FIND PEACE IN YOGA

I am a huge fan of yoga. I love the idea of stretching and strengthening muscles, joints, and ligaments, all while calming and centering my mind. I love that yoga can be done anywhere, at any time, and no equipment is needed.

Keeping our minds and bodies strong, injury free, and limber is critical to our long-term success. How successful can we be if we are spending time in hospitals, doctors' offices, pharmacies getting new prescriptions and ointments, resting, being drugged up on pain killers, going to physio-, chiro-, and massage therapy . . . All that time could be used to get ahead, but instead we use it trying to climb our way up to zero. (I will mention now how much I personally love, appreciate, and respect my chiro- and massage therapist. I use them regularly for prevention of injuries. At times when I had minor injuries, I would spend more than ten hours per week getting myself fixed. Not the best use of my time!)

Being injury free also means I can be a better father because I never need to say no to playing with my kids. It also means being a better husband to my wife, and that's very important (think of how often the slightest injury made you a lump of dough on the coach—not likely being nominated for husband of the year!).

---

* Goggins, David. *Can't Hurt Me: Master Your Mind and Defy the Odds.* (Austin, TX: Lioncrest Publishing, 2018).

An injury has far too many short- and long-term consequences. It has no place in the life of anyone trying to become a world leader. **If you are currently injured, make it priority number one to get healed.** Take the time to get physio-, chiro-, and massage to get yourself back to full health, and immediately start the process of injury prevention (with daily exercise, yoga, healthy eating, etc.).

Hot yoga is my favorite yoga. I think of hot yoga as high-achiever yoga! Hot yoga is yoga done in a hot room; it gets the stretches far deeper because my muscles are far warmer. I particularly love hot yoga because it is a mindset workout above all else.

The whole class you will receive messages from your brain trying to get you to stop, and you have to fight through (within reason here people—if your body is signaling real pain or problems, you listen). My brain tries every trick in the book: "It's too hot in here!" "I can't breathe properly!" "There is too much sweat everywhere!" "Are you crazy?!" It is a beautiful battle, and I win no matter the outcome (even when it's not my best class, I still put in effort, I still stretch it out, and I still sweat like crazy).

Finally, I love all yoga because it forces me to clear my mind and find a peaceful place. Bringing any stresses or work into yoga keeps me tight and uncomfortable. As time passes in yoga, I am forced to focus and be fully present in the moment, leaving all my baggage aside until class is over. The baggage always seems to feel lighter when I go to pick it back up after class, but often I choose to just leave it and walk away carefree.

DRESS TO IMPRESS

"Dress like the person you want to be. Sometimes you have to act
out the person you want to be before you become it."
– JORDAN PETERSON

This might be the simplest, but one of the most effective tips I will give you in this book. When you get dressed tomorrow (for work, school, the gym . . .), dress in the outfit that gives you the most confidence.

You know exactly what outfit I am talking about—the outfit that you put on, look in the mirror, and say, "Dannnnngggggggg, someone is looking gooooood!" This is exactly how you should feel every day. This is the look and feeling you should be hunting for every time you buy an outfit. Don't settle for less. I know these outfits can be difficult to find, but you will simply need to work harder and smarter to find them.

You and I both know that you walk and think with more confidence in this outfit. When you are in this state, do you not believe you are destined to level up in life? Why would we not want this feeling every day?

I am a big fan of dressing above expectations and dressing above your current status. The age-old quote "dress for the job you want, not the job you have" is ultra-valuable advice.

CHALLENGE

Dress way up tomorrow! Go one or two levels above what you normally see with your co-workers. Yes, there is a step too far when you become a distraction (I'm picturing Jim wearing his tuxedo in *The Office*), but don't be afraid to push the limits a bit.

Spoiler alert: when you dress for success, you experience more success. Notice you aren't afraid to make more calls or ask for the sale more confidently. You have better posture all day, you have better energy because you feel better . . .

ADVANCED CHALLENGE

Dress way up all week! Don't just commit to one day, but go all the way. At the end of the week, I want you to take twenty minutes to write down how you felt this week compared to other weeks; successes you experienced; the way others looked at you and treated you; your confidence going into various situations; your relationship with everyone around you. I am confident you will find that it would be silly to go back to your old ways.

These are my favorite quick-change success stories!

If you post about it, please tag #playabiggergame so I can celebrate with you and encourage you to keep going.

MARKUS'S TWENTY-FOUR-HOUR PRINCIPLE

My years with working in baby steps has led me to fully adopt the twenty-four-hour principle. How much can I change in the next twenty-four hours? This is my focal point each day—what impact and change I can make in one day. If I am just 1 percent better today (better with my diet, better as a father, better with my patience, better with my reading, better at my work) then I have succeeded!

In my journey to writing this book, I fell off course badly! I started off so strong and focused. I felt God calling me to write, and as I started I felt like I was on the right path. As I reached the 8,000-word mark, I started to think about where the book was going to go, how much work needed to be done, all the publishers I would need to contact . . . the project became so big that I stopped entirely. I didn't write a single word for almost two months.

Thankfully, God reminded me that He called me to write this book and my next chapter in life wouldn't start until the current chapter was complete. Brooke reminded me of this key principle: to only look at what I can accomplish today.

So I sat back down and committed two hours to writing. It went so well. Now I only focus on what I will write today, what I can achieve today, and the rest of my story will write itself!

One of my favorite stories where this principle is displayed is in the book *Will* by Will Smith. One summer, Will's father had Will and his brother build a wall in front of his father's shop. As you can imagine, two very young boys, stuck inside in the summer, tirelessly working to build this massive wall seemed truly impossible. It would take an eternity. But they started laying just one brick at a time. Nothing else to focus on but just that one brick in front of them. The wall was eventually complete and the beautiful lesson was cemented in for life.

In the big projects of your life, are you staring at an impossible-to-build wall, or are you focusing on just the one brick in your hand? One will stop you from ever taking your first step; the other will move you forward in greater ways than you can imagine.

CHALLENGE

Is there a big project in life you are working on that you feel stalled with? Think about the project in bite-sized pieces. Can you handle one of those small chunks today? Can you handle another small chunk tomorrow?

ADVANCED CHALLENGE

After one week of doing the above challenge, I want you to look back on all you have accomplished for the week. I want you to recall where you started and how you felt looking at the major project. I want you to truly celebrate how far you came in a week. Take an extra minute to pat yourself on the back and spend some time in these endorphins (the endorphins that are released when we feel a sense of accomplishment and take time to celebrate). I want you to crave these endorphins and start looking forward to next week's rush after you complete another seven days of small bites off your project.

It is wonderful to set big goals and go after them. But as you start on the journey, staring at the big goal can often be daunting. Set the goal but focus only on the small pieces—the chunk you can bite off for today. Pretty soon, you will have eaten the whole pie!

"Success isn't overnight. It's when every day you get a little better than the day before. It all adds up."
– DWAYNE "THE ROCK" JOHNSON

STICKY NOTES WILL CHANGE YOUR LIFE

When I started on my path to high achievement, you couldn't find a place in my life that wasn't soaked in sticky notes. I knew that if I wanted to break my old routines—those routines that are so comfortable, require no effort, and have me heading toward a lifeless life, I would need constant reminders of what I should be focusing on and who I should be.

Your assignment today is to go now and buy a packet of sticky notes. You are going to start using them immediately. You will write down key principles, positive phrases, and reminders so your brain will constantly focus on what you want it to focus on.

On my desk right now I have these notes:

"Limits, like fears, are often just an illusion" – Michael Jordan

"Start an Alpha course"

"Let's Sprint"

"You didn't come this far to only come this far."

These notes hit my brain so many times per day that it will now take more work to be lazy and ignore them than to succumb and do as they say.

In the beginning you will want lots of positive messages like: "You're doing great" and "You are better today than you were yesterday!" You will want to add tasks like "Focus on the positive," "Get your workout in today," and "You are in control."

CHALLENGE

Make a few positive notes for yourself now and place them on your work desk, your bathroom mirror, your car, and your nightstand. Be ready to add notes as you read through the other principles to keep yourself on track and accountable. For any new principle/routine/standard/characteristic you are trying to develop/enhance/implement, you should make multiple sticky notes and keep them in places you can't avoid.

ADVANCED CHALLENGE

For the next seven days, write a check mark on each sticky note each day that you accomplish what the sticky note reminded you to do. At the end of seven days, I want you to take the time to celebrate your victories. It is often hard to recognize how far we have come, so racking up those check marks over seven days should open your eyes to how great you are doing. Push yourself to earn those check marks and be deserving of that celebration.

Having these reminders everywhere you turn will keep you focused and on the path to the new, better life you desire.

Post some of your sticky notes and tag us with #playabiggergame so we can learn from you, encourage you to keep going, and celebrate with you!

BULLYING YOURSELF

Earlier in the book I wrote about how my bullies played an important role in making me the man I am today and how I took the advice of Tony Robbins in thanking my bullies. In another chapter we discussed the importance of managing your negative input, as it will negatively impact your every day. Now it is time to look inwardly and talk about how often you are speaking poorly of yourself.

We all have a nagging voice in our head reminding us of our

failures and inadequacies. Some of us have learned to quiet or even silence the voice over the years, but some of us have allowed that voice to gain strength and power and too much influence over our decisions. It is time to take the power back.

When I finally recognized the negative influence my inner voice had over me, I was excited to go to battle. I had silenced my voice in most areas of my life in my twenties, but in my late thirties I realized how loud that voice was as I worked out (when I could have used a supportive spotter more than ever).

Constantly during my workout, that voice would tell me that "you should be much stronger by now" and "for someone who has worked out for as many years as you have, you should have a much better body." I'm not arguing that the voice is wrong, but how does it serve me?

It has been proven over and over that the majority of us will perform far better with someone chanting "you can do it" in our ear than with someone saying "you can't."

Step 1: Recognize that the voice is there.

Step 2: Realize this voice isn't serving you and that it must change.

Step 3: Take the voice over with positive talk!

This is one of the rare times I will encourage you to become a childlike optimist! **I want you to become your own biggest cheerleader.** Since the pendulum is way too far to the negative, we have to bring in a wave of ridiculous positivity to swing it back. I like to think of how Charles Boyle thinks about Jake Peralta in *Brooklyn Nine-Nine*—Jake can do no wrong.

My inner cheerleader thinks I am the greatest guy in the gym ever! "Wow, great set, Markus! How did you even lift that? You are the man!" There is so much praise and positivity that there is simply no room for negativity.

You might ask if this could go too far. Could I become arrogant and cocky outside the gym? Let me reply to that question with two questions: Don't you think you could use a little extra confidence in your life? How much cheerleading do you think it would take you to actually become an arrogant human?

I have found that most people I work with say they start around 6 or 7 out of 10 for confidence. Do you think getting them to an arrogant 11/10 is something that could happen overnight? How much better do you think their lives are with some serious cheerleading that gets them to a 7 or 8 out of 10?

CHALLENGE

In your workout today or tomorrow, before you walk in, channel your inner cheerleader and start the pep rally for yourself! Start right away: "Wow, you are so awesome for getting to the gym today!" Remember to go way overboard and compliment EVERYTHING! "What a great stretch, you must be a professional yoga guy." "You racked those weights like a champ!"

Be consistent. Your cheerleader drank too much pre-workout and is ready to cheer for literally everything for the whole hour you are there. Watch how often you can't help but smile and maybe let out a little laugh. This cheerleader is really obsessed with you.

Do you think this positive feeling will leave you when you leave the gym? Do you need your cheerleader with you for more of your day? Feel free—your cheerleader just had an energy drink and is ready to go!

ADVANCED CHALLENGE

Choose at least one person in the gym today to give a genuine, thoughtful compliment. I would recommend you do not start with the person you think is most attractive. Start with someone you think is awesome for a reason other than looks or physique. Is there someone in the gym who clearly exudes positive energy? That's a beautiful compliment to give. Is there someone who you have noticed is in there consistently? That's a wonderful thing to recognize and compliment on. Is there someone you see there who inspires you? Go tell them, "I know you don't know me, but I just wanted you to know I think you are super inspiring. Thank you for being you."

With all this positive thinking, positive speaking, and positive sharing, there is less room in your life for the negative. **Keep in mind that negative thoughts and attitudes are truly energy draining.** By keeping that out of your life, you will notice you have far more energy in the day, you will think far more clearly, and life will be better.

Recognize and appreciate this change. Enjoy the positive emotions and drink them all in. Take time in this feeling and welcome it back into your life for tomorrow too.

OPTION 2 FOR CHANGING THAT INNER VOICE

When I started writing this section of the book, I thought about who in my life overcame incredible odds and likely had a terrible voice in their head that they had to conquer to get ahead. I immediately thought of my friend Anthony "Showtime" Pettis.

Anthony is the former UFC lightweight champion and has always been known for his exciting, carefree, wild fighting style that earned him multiple "fight of the night," "submission of the night," "performance of the night," and "knockout of the night" bonuses. To fight like that and be the very best in the world, I knew he had done something incredible with that inner voice.

We jumped on a call and I couldn't have loved his answer more!

"I give my inner voice an accent!"

He went on to explain that when we hear our own voice, it's hard to not listen—because it's us.

"Giving the voice a ridiculous accent makes it easy to laugh at it and not take the words as credible."

This is a brilliant concept and a great alternative to going straight to the positive talk. When you hear your negative voice starting up on you tomorrow, give it the craziest accent you can muster and laugh it off! Once you've learned to always give it an accent and dismiss it, fill the void with positive talk in your voice—we both know that's a voice we can trust!

YOUR MIND, THE COMPUTER

Understanding that my mind works very much like a computer has served me well. It is important to know how your mind's systems work so that you don't accidentally get them working against you. When you request that your brain substantiate claims or prove a point, it does so without emotion, just like a computer. It will find the records in your history and experiences that prove you right at all times.

This is your reticular activating system (RAS) at work. As I explained earlier in the book, the RAS filters messages to give your thoughts clarity. Here's a great example—if I ask my mind "Why am I successful?" my mind will look for all the reasons to support why I am successful. It filters out any reasons or thoughts that would lead me to the opposite. It will also become hyper-aware of everything I do in my day that will lead to success. All the answers will be positive.

Sadly, it will work the same if I feed it a negative question. "Why am I such a loser?" My brain will recall all the ways I have failed, the characteristics I don't like about myself, etc. It will also take note of everything I am doing today that further proves my loser status. Even if I do many things in that same day that prove that I am not a loser, the RAS filters it out so I only pay attention to the proof that I am indeed a loser.

This hyper-awareness is an incredible feature of our brains. Have you ever been asked if you see many red cars on the road? You likely haven't noticed one way or another, but now that I just asked you, your brain is going to notify you a thousand times in the next two days every time a red car passes.

Knowing your computer mind works this way, it is imperative to frame questions and comments about yourself with positivity to yield positive answers and thoughts. I am not trying to turn you all into naïve optimists, but I am trying to get you clear of the negative self-talk that plagues the human race and keeps most of us dormant.

CHALLENGE

Ask the following questions to yourself and take time to bask in the wonderful answers you come up with:

Why am I so loved?

What makes me awesomely unique?

Why am I destined for success?

Write your answers down and come back to these questions

tomorrow. Write down all the new answers you have collected since asking the question. Your RAS was working hard to collect the proof.

ADVANCED CHALLENGE

This exercise is going to require some trust and an explanation on why you are doing it and how it works. Do the above challenge with a friend and ask your friend to fill in extra answers as you do the same for them. You are going to love these answers even more than the ones you came up with for yourself!

"There's a part of your brain called the RAS - reticular activating system - and it determines what you notice in the world. When you set a goal, become extraordinarily clear on it and have strong enough reasons behind your intent, you trigger the RAS. Your brain then becomes incredibly acute at noticing anything that comes into your world that could help you move forward, and uncertainty vanishes."
— TONY ROBBINS

Make sure you are using the RAS to your advantage. Ask the right questions. Focus on the positive and what you want in life. When your mind starts asking the negative questions or focuses on the stuff you don't want, catch yourself, call yourself out, and redirect your thoughts so your RAS doesn't take you down the wrong path.

READ MORE

"Education is the most powerful weapon which you can use to change the world."
– NELSON MANDELA

I hope for your sake you are already an avid reader and you don't need anyone to encourage you to read more, but I don't believe studs like you are the majority. For the rest of us, we need constant reminders of the value of reading and learning. I forget to pick up a book and I fall out of my reading routine at times. Know this: there is no easier or faster way to improve your wisdom than to read.

I am a huge fan of modeling. No, not the "Markus on a cover of a fitness magazine" modeling, though I do like that too! I am talking about the modeling concept of finding people who have mastered something and following their path to achieve results far faster than they did. This is why I read.

Someone has spent years, if not decades, working on perfecting their craft. They wrote their instruction manual for us so we can do in three years what took them ten. **I dive into each book with the goal of taking one solid nugget from it.** More often than not, I get more than a handful of brilliant nuggets that dramatically alter the course of my life, but to get just one is worth my investment of time.

To find ultimate success—champion success, greater success than the average person—you must be willing to do far more than the average person. You must exercise your discipline in learning. Some of the most brilliant minds and most successful people in history have put on paper how to achieve their wisdom and success; I would feel foolish suggesting I don't need to read about it.

But that is exactly what we do when we choose not to read the books we have in front of us. Maybe this sounds like a dangerous path to becoming a recluse who does nothing but read and acquire knowledge, but I could sway my pendulum hard toward that side and still get nowhere close to where I would like to be with my intellect and worldly wisdom.

If you find it hard to read or find yourself falling asleep as you read, I have some suggestions for you to turn you into a reader. First, know that I was once exactly like you. Not only did I not enjoy reading, when I did read I often found it boring. It made my eyes so heavy.

Here are some tips to improve your reading experience:

1. **Change the files you created on reading.** If you are like me, I created files when I was very young that said reading was boring. I was being forced to read, and even worse, it was books I had no interest in. So my file said "reading = death by boredom." It took time, but I was able to update my file to "reading = success, wisdom, class, refinement, understanding, influence . . . " You see why I would WANT to read more?

2. **Read books on subjects that interest you.** I'm sure this will be obvious to many of you, but it wasn't obvious to me. I tried reading about so many topics that didn't interest me in the slightest. I got nowhere. But when I first found a book on something that excited me (it was Stephen Covey's *7 Habits of Highly Effective People*), not only did I read it in a weekend, I bought ten copies to give to people I cared about. That book had profoundly changed my life and I wanted the people in

my life to experience it too. Find books on subjects that light you up.

3. **Find authors who have a writing style that works for you.** I was so surprised to realize that not all authors write the same! Some authors use language that melts into my mind like soft butter on warm bread. I can read full chapters without looking up. Other authors were so boring to me that it would take me twenty minutes to get through two pages.

    There is nothing wrong with moving on to the next book if the book you are trying to read isn't working. No one is keeping score of how many you don't finish. People will remember me for my successes, not my failures!

    Find authors that speak to you. Some of my favorite authors: Malcolm Gladwell (*Outliers* shifted my mindset for life), Shawn Achor (I will read everything this man writes! *The Happiness Advantage* is a game changer), Ryan Holiday (*The Obstacle Is the Way*—profound), Tony Robbins (I know, obvious, but that man speaks directly to me every time).

4. **Celebrate/reward yourself with every book you finish.** I have mentioned the value in celebrating all victories, big and small, but especially when you want to reward your brain for doing tasks you want to get excited to repeat. By celebrating after you finish each book (and I mean really do something nice for yourself—maybe you treat yourself to a massage, buy yourself some new shoes, go out for a fancy dinner), your brain will remember that reading equals awesome rewards. You will quickly find yourself eager to jump into the next book.

5. **Ask a friend to join you on the journey.** If you and a friend (or multiple friends) read the same book, you can get into

discussions about it and get far more from the book than what you alone were able to ascertain. More importantly, it will also feed your social needs, and reading can become the path needed for wonderful social time and solid discussions. It will also add accountability. It is great to have a friend counting on you to complete your reading. Your brain will make sure you are reminded regularly to get it done so you don't let others down.

If you are in a book club that is reading *this* book together, please tag me in a post about it with #playabiggergame. Not only will our community encourage and support you, but I would be happy and excited to share your posts and get you some extra recognition! Maybe I will even join you on Zoom the next time your book club meets!

I can't stress enough the importance of reading regularly. They say we only use around 10 percent of our brains, but I am confident that as we learn more about the brain, we will soon discover it is far less than that. It doesn't take much for you to become someone who is using more of their brain that the average human—does it not stand to reason that you will get far ahead by feeding and using yours?

Here are my current top eight book recommendations:

1. *The Happiness Advantage* by Shawn Achor
2. *Awaken the Giant Within* by Tony Robbins
3. *The Power of One More* by Ed Mylett
4. *Outliers* by Malcolm Gladwell
5. *The Obstacle Is the Way* by Ryan Holiday
6. *How to Win Friends and Influence People* by Dale Carnegie
7. *The 7 Habits of Highly Effective People* by Stephen Covey
8. *Good to Great* by Jim Collins

"A reader lives a thousand lives before he dies. . . . The man who never reads lives only once."
– GEORGE R. R. MARTIN

"There is more treasure in books than in all the pirate's loot on Treasure Island."
– WALT DISNEY

"Show me a family of readers, and I will show you the people that move the world."
– NAPOLEON BONAPARTE

"Despite the enormous quantity of books, how few people read! And if one reads profitably, one would realize how much stupid stuff the vulgar herd is content to swallow every day."
– VOLTAIRE

"I was raised by books. Books, and then my parents."
– ELON MUSK

MONEY: DON'T SPEND IT UNTIL YOU HAVE TOO MUCH

"A dollar saved is two dollars earned."
– DAVID CHILTON, *THE WEALTHY BARBER*

I had the great benefit of growing up poor. I learned a lesson about the value of money every single day of my childhood. I saw and felt how painful and stressful it was to fall short every month, even when we had almost no visible "lifestyle" expenses. **Two of the greatest gifts I received in growing up poor are the work ethic to get me out and the fear of ever going back.** These two gifts have given me an incredible level of respect for money.

As with most parents who grew up with little, we don't want our children to face the same pain and stress, and we do all we can to protect them from it. Sadly, with this protection, many of our children have lost the understanding and value of money. Add to this a world that suggests you are only living when you have a Starbucks in your hand, traveling to incredible destinations, snapping photos with your brand-new iPhone, and cruising in your fancy new car and you have a recipe for going back to the poorhouse after just one generation of wealth.

My goal in this section is to relieve financial stress from your life, your children's lives, and ten generations ahead, but also to help all these generations have a better understanding of the value of a dollar. The principle here is very simple, and we are going to make a game out of it. The game is similar to seeing how long you can hold your breath! How long can you make big money without spending it?

Before we go any deeper into this principle, I will clear some things up about it. No, I do not want you saving every penny for tomorrow and never enjoying the fruits of your labor. No, I don't want you to continue to suffer through the poor life, even with money in your account. No, I don't want you to live the Scrooge life and hoard it all. I want to save you from making the same mistake that almost everyone who comes into new money makes—spending it as if it will never stop flowing in and assuming it will only grow from here.

Sadly, I have seen countless friends and colleagues making some money for the first time and immediately spending it on everything they "deserve" for their efforts. "How will the world know I am a shark unless I show my new Range Rover on social media?" said every one of them. The goal of this challenge is not only to stop yourself from spending too quickly, but to become aware that it is a fight between you and the marketers of the world—and only one of you can win.

The marketers of this world are doing better than ever at creating the need for their products. It isn't enough to show it to you and let you make a decision, they will follow you all over the internet and show you their products over and over and over. You didn't even have to search for their product—if you spoke about it anywhere near a device that is hooked up to the internet, it was listening and is ready to market to you.

Once they think they have even a touch of interest, they will also show you people you might know or admire who have already bought their product. **If you don't know that the war exists, you have already lost.**

So my first question to you is this: Are you interested in creating generational wealth or wealth only for you to enjoy? To be clear, there is nothing wrong with choosing the latter, but I want you to be cognizant of the decision and not let someone else make it for you. You may want to just live it up in full and let your children figure it out for themselves. I am going against the grain by saying this, but I fully respect that decision. However, if you want to ensure this new wealth lasts longer than a few years, this principle is as much for you as it is for those who choose generational wealth.

The principle: cut your salary in half and consider that to be how much you are actually making. This principle is going to require incredible discipline, especially because we all believe that everyone on social media is spending like crazy without consequence. The truth is, the consequences are far more severe than we want to realize. According to a 2021 study conducted by Experian, 80 percent of Americans are in debt with an average of over $5,000 in credit card debt, almost $40,000 in student loan debt, and over $20,000 auto debt. This 80 percent does not include the mortgage!

The truth: people can't maintain the spending they show on social media, and it shouldn't be a surprise when they disappear from social media after a couple of years of that lifestyle. I don't want you to become a statistic.

When I cut my income in half and lived on that, it offered far more benefits than just keeping money in my pockets. First, it made me work even harder! You will quickly realize that the $50,000 that comes from your $100,000 in income does not change your lifestyle that much. When I first started making $100,000, I couldn't believe how little I could afford. Guess how motivated I was to get to $200,000.

Second, rainy days never phased me because I had money available. I hope they don't come for you, but rainy days are almost unavoidable. Crap happens in life, from cars breaking down, houses needing repairs, dental work, health stuff . . . things will pop up that require money and you don't want the added stress of not having the money available. I never lost a step due to rainy days.

There was only a small window where I wanted to "show off" my success, but because I lived well under my means, that window was closed before I opened my mouth. I find that people who experience real financial success rarely want to publicly brag about it, and **the people you do see bragging about it publicly are rarely, honestly, financially successful.**

When you start making $500,000 or $1,000,000 in a year, do you really want everyone knowing? Do you really want to paint that target on yourself? Is there any other way for people to see that but bragging? If you do share that information publicly, you are going to experience a new level of loneliness.

I look back so fondly on the early period of this challenge in my life. I remember still driving a Honda Pilot well into my real financial freedom. It ended up being my wife who pushed me into getting a sports car (I chose a Tesla Model S). How many wives push their man into buying the sports car?! Fun side note: at that point, she was still driving a ten-year-old VW Jetta. I think I found the perfect mate.

Finally, mentally cutting your salary in half allows you to invest in a far brighter future. Instead of spending, you have money to invest in new businesses, real estate, stocks, opportunities . . . **If you accept this challenge and stick to it, I am extremely confident you will eventually reach levels of wealth you didn't think people actually reached.**

"The successful among us delay gratification. The successful among us bargain with the future."
– JORDAN PETERSON

Fun Story

In my first five years at Magnum, I didn't take a salary. You read that right: five years. Because I didn't have much money to start the company, I knew that any money I took would stunt its growth. I also knew I would need to build a new discipline (of not spending money like crazy) because money was surely going to come my way.

You might say, "Yeah, but the business probably wasn't worth much or doing much in sales at that point." In year five, we did over $2 million in sales and were handsomely profitable. I stared at those numbers and built discipline.

Not taking a salary for all that time is a key reason why Magnum was able to start buying real estate, was never in scary amounts of debt, and why it was able to grow into the beautiful beast it is today.

Yes, it was challenging. My wife and I didn't go out for dinner often, we weren't buying new clothes, and we checked prices on everything. Brooke will never let me forget that on our tax returns I was her dependant for those years! #truestory

"If you don't save money when you're broke, I'm talking about ten bucks a month, twenty bucks a month, the crazy belief system in the world is that you will save it once you make more. If you have a habit of spending, you will spend more when you make more."
– ED MYLETT

PLAY A BIGGER GAME

BE THE HARDEST WORKING PERSON IN THE ROOM

I'm going to keep this section brief because I know every success-ful person on the planet has said this a million times before. **If you want results in this world that no one else is experiencing, you must be willing to do what no one else is willing to do.** You are in control of your work ethic. You are in control of how you spend your time and your energy. If you want more, you must give more, put out more, exert more, read more, serve more, focus more, dream more, and BE more.

Here is my encouragement to you: you are capable of ten thou-sand times what you think you are capable of. If you work 10 percent harder next week, I know for a fact you will discover you could have worked 20 percent harder. When you step it up again the week after, you will realize it didn't kill you, it didn't wipe you out, it didn't destroy you—you could have done even more. Most people aren't willing to offer even 1 percent extra effort because there are no guar-antees of where it will take you. There is certainly a guarantee, but not the guarantee they were hoping for.

Without putting in the extra effort, I guarantee you a life of mediocrity. I have never met someone at a high level in business, or in life, who didn't, at some point, put in massive effort. Putting in this effort, the extra hours, the additional focus, the added energy will not guarantee success, but you can't get anywhere near that success without first making that investment. It is the cover charge for the good life. If you aren't willing to pay, you aren't welcome to play.

Here is why this is so important to understand—if you believe you deserve success by putting in hard work, you are setting your-self up for discouragement and failure. There's another word for this thought pattern: entitlement. No one owes you anything. God, the universe, the business world—they don't OWE you success because you put in seventy hours of work this week. **If you can understand this principle and learn to love the journey, then you will realize that putting in those seventy hours and showing yourself how disciplined, strong, patient, intentional, driven, ambitious, and hardworking you are IS YOUR REWARD.**

Success is a likely byproduct (and it is far more likely to come to you than someone not putting in your level of effort), but that success will take time. By enjoying the journey, you won't be staring at the clock waiting for it to come. The longer you hang on, the more people who were working hard will start falling away because they didn't learn to enjoy the journey like you did. You will be one of the few left standing and getting to share in the spoils. You will have the biggest smile on your face!

And finally, my reason, my WHY for working so hard—because God did not put me here with a ton of blessings to live a mediocre life. He didn't make you the amazing person you are so you could be really good at watching Netflix! He gave us these gifts, these talents, this wisdom, this experience so that we can change the world. We were sent here to make this world a better place. We were sent here to be great leaders. If I don't put in the work I know I should be putting in, I am letting down my family, my neighborhood, my country, humanity, and God. If that doesn't give you the incentive and motivation to put in extra work, you better check your pulse.

"There will be obstacles. There will be doubters. There will be mistakes. But with hard work, there are no limits."
– MICHAEL PHELPS

CONFIDENCE

As you have no doubt noticed by this point in the book, every mindset tool I have given you, once applied, practiced, and part of your routine, will enhance your confidence.

Discipline and confidence are incredibly intertwined, especially when you have the faith that you are on the right path and that these acts of discipline are daily moving you closer to the success you desire and the human you deserve to be.

In getting a good night's sleep, you can be confident the energy and focus you need will be available to you. You can run your body and mind harder, at its full potential, and be confident it will result in life advancement.

Your morning routine has been created to produce optimal energy for the day, so you can be confident your day is off to the perfect start and you are ready to burst into the world. Since you are now dressed for success and in the outfit that empowers you, you can feel your confidence soaring, as you know you look the part.

Exercise and eating right are my personal biggest confidence contributors. Not only because I know both make me look and feel better every moment of every day, but also because the act of exercising and fueling my body properly are pure self-improvement; and anything I do to improve me is a massive confidence booster. I may be stating the obvious, but people who exercise and eat clean consistently find it easier to stick to it because of how great they look in and out of clothes. Now that's confidence!

Taking the right supplements will give you the confidence that you are maximizing your health and your efforts every day. With more mental capacity and focus, ironclad immunity and illness prevention, and enhanced energy, you know you are able to live each day to its fullest and not be afraid to break through the invisible limits you inadvertently created for yourself.

Knowing that you are already closer to your goals than you were yesterday will give you confidence that you are on the right path and that by tomorrow you will be closer still. For the times when you feel yourself slipping off course, those sticky notes, which you have strategically placed all over your life, will instill confidence by reminding you both how awesome you are and to keep on track.

With your computer-like mind being focused only on the positive, you will be fed confidence all day long and will eventually be convinced that you are more capable than you realized. And because you are feeding your mind with books written by the incredible minds who have already succeeded in ways you desire to follow, you will have more confidence that you know the secret path to get there too.

Add to all of this your work ethic and focus on doing more than others are willing to do and you will have the confidence that success is inevitable.

And finally, by having more money in your hands than your lifestyle requires, you can forget about many, or all, of the financial stresses you once felt. You can be confident in your means to afford this life and your ability to control your finances—not to be controlled by them.

Pro Tip

When I accomplish something, big or small, I take a moment to think about how amazing it is that I did what I did. If you were to do everything I have outlined in this book and took the extra time to recognize how awesome you are for doing it, how could you not be confident? Be confident not only in your likelihood for success, but in everything that makes you you. If you aren't confident in that person, know that I am—and I will bet money on them achieving an incredible amount in this lifetime.

Confidence comes from getting the details right in your daily routine.
The magazine cover is just a perk!

CONSISTENCY

"Nothing in the world can take the place of persistence. Talent will not; nothing is more common than unsuccessful men with talent. Genius will not; unrewarded genius is almost a proverb. Education will not; the world is full of educated derelicts. The slogan 'Press On' has solved and always will solve the problems of the human race."
– CALVIN COOLIDGE

I was so tempted to put consistency far earlier in this book, as I fear many readers will think it ranks last among the seven principles. That couldn't be further from the truth. I could easily rank it first, because **if you don't do these things consistently, you will not succeed.**

I find that consistency is a lost art. I can't say if it is because of short attention spans or the world social media created where we expect results immediately, but I find that the majority of humans start things with great intention and fall off if the results don't come by tomorrow.

I hope I have already given you a taste of success; if you have been doing the challenges in this book, you have noticed significant changes in a short period of time. With consistency over time, that success will be amplified to multiples neither of us can imagine.

At the risk of sounding arrogant, I am Mr. Consistent. I have always found that the longer I stay at something, the more I watch people fall away and I can become the leader who has been at it the longest. If you are only interested in doing something 50 percent, find something else to do. If you aren't willing to put in the full effort, there is almost no chance you are willing to be consistent with it.

Take working out, for example. I have never been the strongest, the most muscular, the one who lifts for hours and hours at a time, or the one who lifts with the most heart . . . but I am the guy you always see in the gym. On one hand I can tell you how many scheduled workouts I have missed in the last fifteen years (and yes, that includes missing a workout due to vacations and illness. I just don't get sick—I also consistently take all my vitamins!). I still might not have the best body on the planet, but I have a body that doesn't get injured, that keeps me healthy, that can do amazing things, and that looks the way I want it to look.

In business, infusing integrity into every decision had one of my businesses ascend slowly, as I was up against competitors who cut corners and had far more margin to offer and more advertising dollars to spend. But staying consistent made my clients take notice of the incredible user satisfaction and the lack of bad press.

When a major news network uncovered a scandal in our industry, with thirty-nine out of the forty brands tested complicit in the scandal, you better believe my brand stood out as the only one listed as doing it right! It may have taken longer than I had hoped to sell a million dollars in product, but you can imagine the satisfaction when we reached $150 million in sales, through over one hundred countries, without compromising our integrity.

Without consistency, you can only get a taste of success and progression. In staying consistent, you can feast on prosperity for life.

IT'S NOT ABOUT THE DESTINATION: LEARN TO ENJOY THE JOURNEY

Being goal oriented and focused is far from a bad thing! It is so important to set our goals so we know both where we are going and when we arrive. But it is of even greater importance to set a path toward your goal that you will enjoy.

So many colleagues I have known over the years have learned this the hard way. They knew their goal well, but chose to adopt the "do whatever it takes" mentality to get them there. Without fail, that road ended early and in sadness and confusion. **Finding the right path for you is as important as or more important than setting your goal.**

If we do achieve the goals we set for ourselves but don't enjoy the journey, or if we create a path that isn't aligned with our core values, achieving the goal can easily be a sour achievement instead of a victorious moment.

Here's an obvious example: You had the goal of winning a race. When no one was looking, you were able to cheat and win by great lengths. How good does that victory feel? You may receive the medal, but you are now forever cursed with watching your back and wondering if someone found you out. You will always know what you did.

Fun fact: the longer it takes to achieve a goal, the greater the taste of victory with integrity and the more sour the taste of victory without it.

Once you know your goal, you need to take the time to plot out all the ways to get there and keep an open mind to new routes as you go along in your quest. Foolish is the man who does not accept the new knowledge and sticks only to what he knew in the beginning. How did that work out for Blockbuster Video?

Learning to enjoy the journey can be a beautiful process! "I earned a million dollars" is not the story you want to tell. "How I earned a million dollars" is the story we all want to hear. If you set your mind to finding the beauty in your journey, you will find so much joy in life, and the success will be the cherry on top. **Fun truth: the more you enjoy your journey, the far more successful you will be.**

> "For me, happiness is the joy we feel striving after our potential."
> – SHAWN ACHOR

CONSISTENTLY USE YOUR FILTERS

No, I am not talking about Snapchat filters, I am talking about the filters you have now created from doing the exercises in this book.

Does the decision line up with your faith? Will this decision serve you or others? Does this decision act on gratitude? Is this a disciplined decision? As you consistently filter your decisions, they will become easier to make. You will subconsciously create routines for decision-making and your life will daily get closer to perfect alignment.

These decisions will also have the beautiful side effect of removing the wrong people and situations from your life and attracting the right people and situations. The more consistent you are, the greater the magnetic pull you will have for the things in life you desire most. Even your desires will submit to the new you, and you will ultimately find yourself desiring the things that keep you on the right path.

In the same way that people can negatively spiral out of control when putting themselves in the wrong situations by making poor decisions, you will find yourself in a positive vortex; it will take more effort to get out of positivity than to stay in it.

DON'T GET COMPLACENT

As you travel down this beautiful path, there will be times where you will be tempted to let your guard down. Don't! It is human nature to get complacent and allow pride to give us a sense of invincibility. You will need to constantly remind yourself that while you are going left, the whole world is going right, and you can be carried away by the current when you least expect it.

The path less traveled will always require focus and effort. The path everyone else travels is smoothed out and requires almost no effort at all, but you will be rewarded in direct correlation to the effort you invest. **The more consistently you are consistent, the easier being consistent becomes.**

At least once every month, take time to look back on how your month went. How are you doing with all these principles? Are you remembering to celebrate all the victories? Are there areas you have let slip and need to reinvest in?

Ed Mylett, in his amazing book *The Power of One More*, talks about getting comfortable with being inconvenienced. There is no success to be found on the path of convenience. "A fundamental truth about life is that convenience and greatness cannot coexist."

Think about any time in your life where you truly jumped ahead. It could have been with your workouts, your career, your relationships. Remember what it took to get ahead. It took extra effort and discomfort. It took extra time, extra energy, extra focus. Were those workouts easy? Did sticking to your diet require almost no effort? Did enhancing your relationship require no time or focus? Of course you had to put in extra, but it was well worth it.

It's never a bad time to start fresh and recommit your efforts. This is a great time, right now, to look back on the successes you have had in taking on the challenges in this book. Did you discover that you are stronger and more disciplined than you realized? Use this and be confident in who you are and the path you have chosen—you are on your way to greatness!

> "The tragedy of life is often not in our failure, but rather in our complacency; not in our doing too much, but rather in our doing too little; not in our living above our ability, but rather in our living below our capacities."
> – BENJAMIN E. MAYS

ENERGY GAINERS AND DRAINERS

Here's one more filter to add to your arsenal: What would happen if we viewed everything in life as an energy-gainer or an energy-drainer?

Whether we recognize it or not, we fill our day with energy-drainers, then wonder why we are absolutely wiped by 3 p.m. If we think of our daily energy as a tank of gas, we need to be conscious of where we are blowing through our fuel, what we can do to top up the tank, and the importance of refueling every night with great sleep.

Be mindful of items on your list that don't just drain your energy but poke holes in the tank! These can be extra dangerous and must be monitored or more than just your energy will be thrown off. (Ever been in a really bad fight with your significant other? Were you able to put that aside as you went about your day, or did it absolutely wipe your energy every second that passed? It is in your best interest to immediately resolve the issue so you can get back to your high-achieving ways.)

Here's what I find extra interesting about this concept: every person's list will be unique to them. What might drain my energy might fill you up! It is important to know what things in your life drain you and what fill you up so that you can create a proper balance and be in control of your energy levels.

I recently recognized a frequent internal struggle I was having between reading and watching TV. Reading is an energy-gainer to me. I love self-improvement (shocker, I know), I love learning, I love setting a good example for my daughters, and I love that it makes my wife even more attracted to me (she digs a man who reads).

Watching TV on the other hand is a major energy-drainer for me. Programming is so bad these days and I feel gross sitting there. Not only do I not enjoy what I am watching, but I also feel lazy, think less of myself for watching instead of reading, set a bad example for my children, and turn my wife off! Easy decision, right? But other variables often come into play and old stories can easily take over. For me, my old file on TV sometimes shows up and says TV is fun and relaxing. Plus, the TV is right here, and my book is way over there! Knowing what's on your list is powerful.

Take a moment to list out your energy-drainers and your energy-gainers.

Drainers

_____

_____

_____

_____

_____

_____

Gainers

_____

_____

_____

_____

_____

_____

_____

The purpose of this list is not to clear all energy-drainers out of your life—that could be a futile task, and I think there would be many young children left without parents! (Come on, I figured I have built up enough rapport with you to make a joke! I love my children, but go ahead and tell me raising a two-year-old isn't draining!!)

This is such an important list for you to know so you can recognize and explain why on certain days you are wiped, and on other days you are overflowing with energy. It is also a wise move to add energy-gainers each day, so you never pull up to the house on fumes. I find it incredibly valuable to book full days, once in awhile, that are full of only energy-gainers! As you look over your list, I am confident you have a big smile on your face as you imagine a day full of those beautiful things!

COMMUNICATE, COMMUNICATE, COMMUNICATE

"Communication is a skill that you can learn. It's like riding a
bicycle or typing. If you're willing to work at it, you can rapidly
improve the quality of every part of life."
– BRIAN TRACY

I owe a great deal of success to my unwavering commitment to
communication. If you ever wonder if you are not communicating
enough, you are not. If you wonder if you communicated something
thoroughly enough, you did not. If you wonder if you should increase
your communication, you should. I have yet to find a scenario where
my increased communication got me in trouble.

Before I get into the meat of this juicy principle, I will add the
caveat that this principle must be accompanied by the mind of a
learner. If you do not have the mind of a learner, the extra communication will be mostly the same questions and conversations on
repeat, and no one has the patience for that.

If I have a question about how to do something, I ask it. I don't
stop to think of how others will view me by asking or if it is the
correct time to ask. I just ask. As an employer, I tell every one of my
staff on their first day that I will never get mad at them for asking
how to do something if they don't know how. **Asking takes guts and
initiative.** (If you have to ask the same question twice because you
didn't listen the first time, we have a different problem.)

If you don't know how something works, ask. If you are unclear
with instructions, ask. Wondering how that made someone feel,

wondering if that came across the right way, wondering someone's opinion or thoughts . . . I think you see where I am going with this.

Since I devoted my life to being an over-communicator, I can't help but notice that 99 percent of all movie conflicts are created by lack of communication or a miscommunication. I suppose one could argue that 99 percent of conflicts wouldn't exist if they took on this principle; or at the very least, 99 percent of movies wouldn't exist!

In being a clear communicator, I have no time or patience for passive-aggressiveness. If you have this in your arsenal, I suggest you remove it immediately. Most people in high-power positions will not tolerate it for a second.

Passive-aggressiveness is purposely unclear, gives mild hints instead of being direct about a need or complaint, expresses anger and disappointment without directly communicating it, purposely fails or doesn't deliver on promises to prove a point, silently keeps score, gives backhanded compliments, insists conflict is resolved without letting go . . . man I feel gross just listing this stuff.

I don't want you to feel picked on, but if you do any of these things, stop. I promise you, I have never met someone with power using any of these techniques. Let me rephrase that, I have never seen someone stay in power if these techniques are in their arsenal.

Being a strong communicator has taken me far, has built incredible, honest relationships, and has gotten me out of some very tricky situations. Be consistent in your clear communication and be diligent in finding clarity—you will find it far easier to stay in integrity and will find far fewer gray areas in life.

CONSISTENTLY EATING RIGHT

I can't possibly harp on this point enough—you can't get anywhere near your body or mind's potential without fueling them properly.

Fueling your body properly must be a daily practice. I hope you stick to the challenges long enough to recognize how amazing your body and mind can feel if they are fueled properly every day. I hope you take the time to reset the bar as to how you want to feel every day, then proceed to do what needs to be done to get you there.

Fun Story

My unique eating habits have created story after story, and I am 100 percent confident it will do the same for you! I have already told you how my clean eating caught the attention and affection of the woman I would spend my life with, but I want to share with you some of the crazy hijinks it has got me into as well. **Like the time twenty heavily armed security guards were hunting me down in the airport!**

I was on a typical business trip and, as always, I had my food with me in my carry-on. Because I sweat so much with my cardio and training, I use quite a bit of salt for replenishment; plus, I really like salt. I happened to have a full shaker of salt with me on this trip.

As I went through the X-ray, they pulled me over for an extra check. The agent barely looked at my stuff and said I was good to go. I remember it seeming so strange to me that he barely looked, but he gave me the green light, so away I went.

I walked for almost ten minutes to my gate and saw a delay in my flight, so I started walking back to the area where the shops were. As I walked, I saw teams of men holding very large guns going by, like something serious was going down. I first saw two teams of three men, then another set of six going by me at a fast jog—this was a real threat.

Next, I saw a group of soldiers and agents, these guys looked like secret service with their fancy black suits and ties and ear pieces—I had never seen these guys in an airport before. They locked eyes with me, pointed, and moved in.

Fortunately, I know I am an upstanding citizen and had no reason to fear, so I calmly asked, "What's going on?" In classic secret service/ *Men in Black* fashion, they wouldn't say, but told me to follow them. It was surreal being led by two well-dressed secret agents, plus six heavily armed guards encircling me, all the way back to the security checkpoint. I imagined my pastor or clients seeing me being led away like I was a massive terrorist threat!

This all happened because of the saltshaker. Because salt is an organic substance, it needs to be triple-checked at security because it registers in the X-ray the same as many bomb-building materials would. (To be honest, I am going off memory here—please remember my heart rate was slightly elevated at this point!)

I know some of you will read that story and say, "That sounds like my worst nightmare! I am not ever bringing food through security!" But I LOVE a good story to tell and feel blessed to be part of these shenanigans. Do also remember, it wasn't the food that set this off, it was the salt. I have been through security hundreds of times with a crazy amount of food and almost never had an issue, so don't let my fun story deter you from making good decisions!

THE VALUE OF A COACH OR MENTOR

In reading this book and putting everything you have learned into practice, you are well on your way to a far more successful life. However, we are human and we will likely stumble; we may regress and we may forget our way at times. **I can't encourage you enough to get a coach and a mentor in your life to keep you on track.**

If you were looking to change your body, and you read a book about how to exercise and started doing it, do you see the added value in someone making sure you were doing the right movements and how many and to keep you accountable on your journey? Do you see the value in listening to someone who was once in a similar position to you, but has radically changed their body over time and is willing and able to teach you what they did? This person will also help keep you from injuring yourself and teach you how to avoid the most common pitfalls. If you haven't found that value yet, the right coach will get you there in, at most, half the amount of time compared to doing it alone.

Whether you are training your body or your mind, having someone there who is qualified and whose sole purpose in your relationship is to get you further on your path faster and more efficiently is of massive value. Don't forget this: once you get to a new level in physique or with your mind, you will see that the levels are unlimited, and each level comes with exponentially greater benefits! The faster you level up, the greater the rewards for life.

Who is qualified and how do you find them? If you have read this far, I am confident you have some trust in me and my discernment. For over twenty-five years I have surrounded myself with the best of the best in both the physical and mental realms. If you come to playabiggergame.com, you will find the right people. I would love to be the one to introduce you to those who will elevate your life, and I would love to be part of that journey too! My people are chosen not only because they get results, but also because they do it with integrity and without sacrificing anyone's health. Come and join our community today and let's push each other to great new heights.

> "If you are committed to achieving the level of lasting results you desire and deserve in your life, you need a proven game plan, outstanding coaching, and an immersion experience that will compress decades into days."
> – TONY ROBBINS

HAVE A PLAN—ALWAYS

If you want long-term, consistent results, you must always have a plan. Every one of the principles in this book requires focus and intention if you want to see the fruits of your labor. Without a plan in place, it will be easy to get derailed and to blame others for your lack of control.

I learned early in my journey that I needed to visualize my day, every day, if I wanted to live this new life to its fullest. If you simply "go with the flow," you will find it near impossible to achieve what you are looking to achieve. Don't forget, the "flow" represents what everyone else is doing; if you get caught in that wave, I promise you will find it going in the opposite direction of where you want to go.

Let's talk examples. If you want to consistently eat properly for your goals, you must always know where your next meals are coming from and when. Early in my journey I was constantly caught unprepared because a meeting ran long, the restaurant someone chose had no healthy options, there were no restaurants near us, etc. Trust me, without a plan, your eating choices will be made for you, and 9/10 times it will be far from healthy.

Without a plan, going out with friends made me break multiple rules every time! There was almost no chance I was eating the right foods at the right times, but I was also staying out too late because I had no way home when I wanted to leave, maybe partaking in more alcohol than I'd prefer because I didn't plan one way or another, or being put in a position where my safety or integrity could be called into question.

Travelling without a plan will cause you major setbacks. Whether it be for business or pleasure, I always investigate and have my plans for working out, eating right, and getting good sleep. Don't assume the hotel you are staying at has a decent gym; confirm it. Don't assume you will have healthy food available to you; confirm it and pre-order meals if need be. Don't assume you will get a good sleep; make plans to make it so.

I could go through every principle in this book and show you why planning is critical for your embodiment of each. Truly successful people are always looking a couple of steps ahead so they can see the pitfalls coming and make plans to avoid them.

This is a simple process—take five to ten minutes in the morning, while you are getting your morning walk in perhaps, to visualize how the day will go. Where will you be at mealtimes? What will you eat? Who will you be around? Are your power clothes clean and ready to wear? Are you ready to encourage, to be patient, merciful, respectful, grateful? Making the plan is a key step in your daily routine to maximize your chances for success.

80 YEARS • A LEGACY OF INFORMATION INSPIRATION TRANSFORMATION • 1936–2016

IRON MAN

INSANE
BICEPS
PUMP

MAN UP
SECRETS OF
TESTOSTERONE

BACK ATTACK
BIG & WIDE

TURN CARBS
INTO MUSCLE

MAY 2016

$6.99US $7.99CAN

05>

0 73361 08014 1

PLEASE DISPLAY UNTIL 05/31/16

EASY ABS FOOLPROOF
CORE TRAINING

Consistency is what allows me to keep pushing
boundaries and finding success.

EPILOGUE

As I wrote these pages, I spent wonderful time in deep discussion with some brilliant humans, and I found myself more committed than ever to living by these principles daily. I recognize how critical it is to spend time with like-minded people to learn how to further understand and execute this glorious stuff in my life.

One reason I have been so devoted to these principles for so long is knowing that for my first fifteen years, I lived the exact opposite of them all and all I had to show for it was pain and failure. I had and used every excuse to get out of hard work. I surrounded myself with enablers who helped me dig my trenches. I told myself stories about why I wouldn't succeed in life and how I was undeserving of a good one. Spoiler alert, I got exactly what I deserved—nothing.

Just remembering myself speaking those stories and excuses leaves a terrible taste in my mouth today and makes me strive even harder toward greater things. **Success in any area of life is a choice.**

HOW WILL YOU USE YOUR NEW INFLUENCE?

With this book, I am handing you a massive source of power and influence. I hope I've done a solid enough job in my writing and encouraging that you will wield this power and influence for good, to serve humanity.

The more success you experience in your life, the stronger your influence grows. The more that people see you getting ahead in life, the more they will come to you for advice and, more importantly, put that advice into practice immediately. This is real influence.

It is also important to recognize that your actions speak far louder than your words, so living a life of integrity is now more critical than ever. You are accountable to millions for your actions. I hope you don't see that as added pressure, but instead embrace the account- ability, because living a life of integrity is what you truly want. The accountability is a reminder that there is more at stake than just what we desire in any given moment.

GO!

You now have a toolbox full of powerful tools that you can use to change your story. It is now on you to consistently use these tools and exercise these principles.

Not regularly exercising what you've learned and hoping for great success is like never working out and hoping to wake up one day with the perfect body. You are more likely to win the lottery without buying a ticket! You have the knowledge, you have the drive (you read this far, didn't you?), you have the story, and you have the ability; now it is up to you to step into your destiny. **Your success is waiting for you to claim it. Your success is inevitable.**

Now GO! Become the person this world needs you to be. Become the person your children, your partners, your associates, your fans are proud of. Become greater than even the person you always dreamed of becoming. **You are far more powerful and amazing than you know, and now you have the wisdom to move ahead in life.**

Don't stop. Don't slow down until you achieve everything you have ever wanted to achieve and then some. You are a gift to this world, and I am beyond grateful to have been on this journey with you.

ONE LAST REQUEST

One last request—a favor to me. **The greatest gift you can give to me is making a decision, right now, to change the course of your life. Decide that your story changes right this very second.**

Write your new story, then do everything you can to make that success story come to fruition. Picture the conversation we will one day have, of you telling me how you changed your life. Picture me telling your story to my future audiences, and maybe even writing it in my next book. Use that image daily to keep you on course and push outside your comfort zone, to make your story even greater than you imagined!

Nothing lights me up more than having people come up to me and tell me that they heard me speak, came to a seminar, or read my work months ago, made that change, and can't believe the path they are on today because of it. **You can be a success story—it is your choice.**

Finally, know that I am praying for you. I have been praying for you since I started writing this book. I pray you feel empowered, that you recognize how amazing you are and what you are capable of. I pray that you have the faith and confidence in yourself to show up every day and give your best. I pray that you go forth from this moment and that your life and your whole world change in ways you can't even imagine.

ACKNOWLEDGMENTS

Let's start with the most amazing wife on the planet. Brooke makes me believe I am the most handsome, manly, confident, well-built man of integrity and that anything less than unimaginable success would be a shocking outcome. I am forever yours, Brooke. I was made for you, and you are God's gift to me. I plan to prove that to you every day as long as I still have breath in me.

To my Claire-Bear, my Cubby. You are remarkable. Your discipline, wisdom, kindness, social intelligence, and understanding of having a life-calling is like nothing I have ever seen in a young woman. I can't wait to see the woman, mother, wife, and world leader you become. If you stay on this path and continue to grow the way you have, I am 100 percent certain you will create the exact life that you choose to have. It is such an honor to be your father.

To my Bailey-B. I love your energy and your spirit. I love how you love. You have been gifted with a generous, humble, others-first nature, and you are an incredible gift to this world. I know that you will lead and influence at such a high level and will change lives everywhere you go. When you apply yourself, the world bends to your desires. I am so proud of you for the effort you put into your passions, and I couldn't feel more blessed to be your dad.

To Brian and Heather Larsen. Bless you two for the massive impact you have had on my life. From the beginning, you saw the brokenness in me, but you also saw something good. You offered me love like I had never seen it offered before. You accepted me as a son from day one and I will be forever grateful. But more importantly, you created and nurtured the most wonderful woman to ever walk the planet, and you trusted her hand in mine. Thank you for being amazing parents and showing me what Christian parents can look like.

To my long-time mentor, Tony Robbins. I know that I would not be the Markus I am today without you. Since I was fifteen years old you have kept me accountable to the man you know I can become. I am forever grateful for your wisdom and your obedience to your calling to teach, encourage, shape, and transform the leaders of this world. I have tried to and forever will aspire to make you proud of me.

To my best friend, coach, and brother, Darren Kaulius. What an incredible story God is writing in our lives, eh brother? I am so proud of you. You have evolved so miraculously in the last few years and I am so excited to witness you become the man you were always destined to be. I am grateful for every moment we get to spend together. Thank you for challenging me to constantly grow and question my assumptions and mindset. Thank you for helping me work out so many concepts in this book. We are going to light this world on fire, brother.

To my long-time business partner, Rodney Jang. Thank you for being a great business partner, challenging me, and giving me space to grow. Thank you for the trust you have put in me and for the faith in business partnership that you restored in me. It is an honor and pleasure to be your partner and friend. I love seeing you flourish in your role at BioEdge—the role you were always meant to play.

Thank you to the mentors in my life who challenge me to think bigger every day. Thank you, Ed Mylett, Jon Gordon, David Meltzer, Craig Siegel—you men are titans who set a beautiful standard for living my greatest life, serving and giving more without any expectation of receiving. Most importantly, you know how to love without hesitation and without limit. Thank you for the contributions you have made to my life and this world.

Thank you to the mentors of my earlier years. You invested in me before most people would invest in me. Thank you, Paul Bodnarchuk, Aaron LaBarre, Bernie Ferbey, and Phillipe-Antoine Defoy—you guided me, talked through tricky situations with me, and shared your wisdom and friendship with me. I will not forget that.

Thank you, Brian Buhler, my spiritual mentor, my friend, and my father-figure. You may never know how massive of an impact you have had in my life. I have looked up to you and respected you so much since the moment I met you. The way you looked into my soul and knew that God had something far bigger planned for my ministry forever changed me. I knew that you believed in me in that moment, and I will work until my last breath to prove you right. Don't think I've ever forgotten the profound insight that you gave to me straight a long time ago: "Markus, don't believe your own hype."

To the Pettis brothers, my guys. Anthony and Sergio, I am so proud of you both for becoming such massive leaders. I am so grateful for your friendship. You guys have kept me young, and I respect you both so much for your work ethic, your lack of fear, and your limitless mindset for what you believe you can achieve. You two are true entertainers and warriors in every respect, and you deserve all the success coming to you.

To my sisters, Karen and Julie. You have played unique roles in my life. Julie, I am sorry I never made more of an effort in our relationship. I appreciate your energy when I get to see you, and I am praying for you and your family constantly. Karen, you played the mother role in my life for many years, and I am so grateful for that. You showed me so much love over the years. I hope you will look back on your tough times and see me standing with you and encouraging you through.

To my mom. I will start by apologizing for all the years I wasn't a good son, and I know there were quite a few. I'm also sorry for not devoting more time to having a personal relationship with you. I am so grateful for the mother you were to me. I learned so much about independence and strength because of you. Thank you for being my mom and for playing that role perfectly for me.

That brings us to you, dad. I sure hope you read these pages and see the love and respect I have for you. I apologize for comparing you to what my young mind thought a dad should be. I'm sorry for the role I played in the conflict we had for so many years. I am so grateful for the father you were. I pray we can grow closer together.

To my *Mocuite*, Zita Kaulius, the strongest woman I knew. It has been years since she left this earth, but her work here, her legacy, will carry on forever. It was my *Mocuite* who poured extra love into my life during the divorce. Even at that age, I knew she was going way out of her way to make sure I felt loved. It was my *Mocuite* who grabbed my hand after church one day and said, "come with me, you're giving your life to Jesus." My *Mocuite* didn't believe in the made-up limitations we put on ourselves. The proof is in her unbelievable life story.

To Rory and AJ Vaden, Jeremy Weber, Elle Petrillo, and the whole Brand Builders Group, a thousand thank-yous! I have loved working with you and I am so happy God connected us. What you do to help people build their personal brands and for authors launching their books is unmatched. This book would not be where it is today without you. I hope to be one of your favorite success stories.

To Naren Aryal, Myles Schrag, Will Wolfslau, and Amplify Publishing Group. Thank you for believing in me and bringing your energy to this book project! I feel like the work has just begun, and I am excited to be on this journey with you. I hope my book brings your company the attention and success you deserve.

To all my business buds who challenged me, broke bread with me, shared laughs with me, and helped me to learn business. I owe you so much. Ruan, Leigh, Derick, Brad, Brad, Brad (LOL), Dan, Brady, Ben, Nathan, Shaun, Jason, Jason, Jason (now it's just getting silly!), Cam, Chris, Jeff, Geoff, Brian, John, Matt, Keith, James, Allan, Nicole, Dave, Dave, Paul, Ipe, Terri, Travis, Peter, Devon, and Tom Tardi and Richard Pierce, thank you for making that chapter in my life so exciting and fun!

To my high school drama teacher, Barb Barker. I can't thank you enough for getting me out of my shell. There was something about the way you looked at me that made me know that you knew I could be someone awesome. I will never forget you for that or cease being grateful for you and how awesome you are.

To Micah LaCerte and Diana Chaloux-LaCerte. You are two of my favorite people. I love you both so much. I am so grateful God has aligned us for so many years and that we are now being placed on the same path. You two inspire me and millions of others to work harder and devote more of our lives to God's will. I am so proud of you both and I am so blessed to have front row seats to the miracle that is your lives.

Thank you to the amazing group of friends who push me daily to grow and become a better version of myself. Jean Jacques Barrett, Zack Taylor, Brett Barker, Mathew Park, Randy Molland, Sach Latti, and Jake Fleshner—I need you good men with me on this journey and I am so blessed to know each of you. Thank you for the role you are playing in my life.

Thank you to all my old-school, high-school buddies. Dave Camara, Brandon Thomas, Jared Hulme, Joel Hulme, and Brian Wilson, you guys were there for me when I didn't believe I deserved anyone. I am so grateful for you, and I am starting to feel a little bad about being so aggressive with our hockey card trades.

Jordan Taylor, you get your own shoutout! You were my best friend at a time when I felt I had no one. I loved growing up with you, brother. Thank you for your part in giving me the life I have— you had a major role. Thank you for being a good man, a great friend, and for always carving out space for me in your life.

To the millions of people (wow, millions sure is a big word) who have supported me and my growth over the years, thank you! You believed in me enough to buy my products, watch my videos, leave encouraging messages, vouch for me, pray for me, and one way or another send love my way. I am so grateful for every one of you, and I hope you feel the love coming back your way right now.

I would have nothing and be nothing without my generous Holy Father in heaven, His amazing Son Jesus, and His Holy

Spirit. Thank you, Lord, for forgiving me and setting me free from the prison of sin and guilt. Thank you for instilling in me and equipping me with the gifts and talents to carry out the plans you have for my life. Thank you for being with me every moment of every day and allowing me to experience your unmeasurable power. I pray that people will not remember or even see me as I carry out your will but rather see only you. Your will be done, Lord, not mine.

Φ

PLAY A BIGGER GAME

ABOUT THE AUTHOR

Markus Kaulius is a serial entrepreneur and the founder of multiple eight- and nine-figure businesses. In a career of more than twenty-five years, he has grown his supplement company from a startup to $170 million and helped clients worldwide lose more than three million pounds. As a thought leader in the business and health industries, he advises multiple eight- and nine-figure companies on growth strategy and has been featured in major media such as PBS, Fox News, and CNN. With an online following of over 300,000, Kaulius shares daily insights with his community, spanning business strategy, mindset, health, and most importantly of all, faith. Through his new venture, playabiggergame.com, Kaulius is bringing together the world's greatest minds and sharing lessons learned from his entrepreneurial journey to help other high achievers break free from imbalance and feelings of discontent and inadequacy so they can find fulfillment beyond career success.

@MARKUSKAULIUS @MARKUSKAULIUS

@MARKUSKAULIUSPLAYBIG